STERLING SILVER HOLLOWARE

Distributed by Charles Scribner's Sons, New York

Sterling Silver Holloware

Tea and coffee services, pitchers and ewers,
bookmarks, ash trays, candelabra, salts and peppers,
desk sets and dressing sets, berry bowls, napkin rings,
cups, tea balls and bells, trays, flasks, match safes

GORHAM MANUFACTURING CO., 1888
GORHAM *MARTELÉ*, 1900
UNGER BROTHERS, 1904

Edited, with an historical introduction by Dorothy T. Rainwater

AMERICAN HISTORICAL CATALOG COLLECTION

THE PYNE PRESS
Princeton

First edition
Library of Congress Catalog Card Number 72-95726
SBN 87861-041-3, paperbound edition
SBN 87861-040-5, hardcover edition

Catalog material used in assembling
Sterling Silver Holloware courtesy
of The Gorham Co., Division of Textron,
Providence, Rhode Island

Introduction material courtesy
of Samuel Kirk & Sons, Baltimore,
Maryland

MANUFACTURED IN THE UNITED STATES OF AMERICA

Sterling Silver Holloware

an historical introduction

Through the centuries silver has determined the destinies of men and changed the shape of nations. The word itself comes from the Old English *seolfor*, akin to Old High German *silabar* or *silbar*, the Old Norse *silfr*, and the Gothic *silubr*, all of which came from a prehistoric Germanic word borrowed from an Asiatic source. Numerous references to silver are found in the Bible where it is most often mentioned in connection with the decoration of the tabernacle in the wilderness (Exodus), in the building of King Solomon's temple (I Kings) and the temple in Jerusalem (Ezra). The arts of the silversmith were well known in Biblical times as were the techniques used in refining the metal. The fining pot for silver is used as a familiar image (Proverbs 17:3). From archaeological evidence as well as the earliest records, silver was used as a medium of exchange, for personal adornment, for useful vessels and as a token of wealth.

It is generally conceded that the first metals discovered and used by early man were gold, copper and silver, in that order. Silver was probably discovered after gold and copper since it is less abundant in the pure metallic state. It is often not easily recognizable, being normally found as a sulphide in ores. Present studies indicate that the earliest known metal mines were worked by pre-Hittites in Cappadocia in the eastern part of Asia Minor apparently some time in the fourth millennium B.C. Ore deposits were later exploited in Armenia and Bactria, and westward to the Aegean Sea. About 500 B.C. the silver-lead mines in Greece, at Laurium, southeast of Athens, were among the rich mines of antiquity. From the Isle of Man to the Mediterranean, silver was mined in ancient times, with the Roman mines in what is now Spain being the richest. The output of these mines paled, however, beside those of the New World. Not only were the mines of Mexico, Bolivia and Peru much larger but the ore was richer in silver than the European.

Then came the discovery of tremendous new silver sources in the Sierra Nevada in the United States. Soon after the accidental discovery, in 1859, of the colossal Comstock Silver Lode, on the eastern slope of Mount Davidson in Nevada, the United States was established as the largest producer of silver—a lead retained until about 1900. This vein was discovered by two men who had been lured west after the California gold rush of 1849. As they worked for gold on the claim along the Carson River, they tossed aside some odd-looking, heavy blue rock as worthless. Henry Comstock, trapper and fur trader, recognized the blue rock and staked a claim adjacent to theirs. A rich silver ore, the blue rock assayed almost $4,000 a ton. In February, 1873, that giant ore body, the "Big Bonanza," was struck in the district of the "silver mountains" in the California and the Consolidated Virginia mines. No single silver lode has ever poured forth wealth at such an astounding rate.

Today, most of the world's silver comes from mines in the western mountain regions of North America. Silver is a soft metal, far too soft in its pure state to be used for most purposes. From the earliest days, silversmiths have alloyed it with other metals to harden it, and long ago found copper the most satisfactory metal for this purpose. The British sterling standard, with its proportions of 11 oz. of pure silver to 18 dwts. of copper per pound troy (.925),

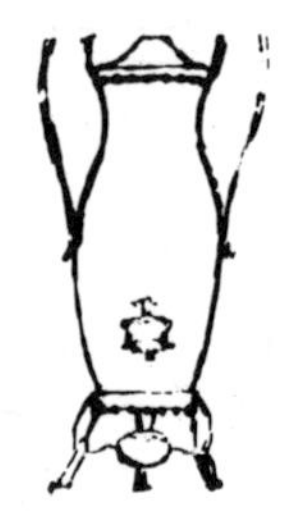

The way in which silversmiths dealt with customers before the advent of mass production is illustrated in these sketches of an urn, prepared for Mrs. James Wadsworth of Geneseo, N.Y., by S. Kirk in 1851. Mrs Wadsworth chose the urn on the right.

has been used at least since the early fourteenth century, and probably since Anglo-Saxon times. The word *sterling* is believed to have been derived from the "Easterlings," coiners from East Germany whom Henry II hired to improve the coinage of his realm. The term "Easterling silver" was later abbreviated to "sterling silver," and the term has come down through the centuries as a mark of high quality.

Virtually no silver bullion from native ores was available to American silversmiths before the great mid-nineteenth century silver strikes. It is generally conceded that the metal used in the seventeenth centuries was obtained by melting down coins or objects that had gone out of fashion. Maintaining the sterling standard posed no problem if the objects melted down were of English origin because of that country's strict quality control. Coins were another matter. The currency used in the colonies was chiefly from England, Spain and Portugal. Evidence indicates that the bulk of American silver of colonial times was made from melted down Spanish coins which were .900 fine, a 25 parts poorer mixture than sterling. (American coins from 1792 till 1837 were of even lesser quality, .8924, but after January 18, 1837, American silver coinage was of .900 fineness until the advent of "sandwich" coins.)

From the year 1300, it has been compulsory in England to guarantee the quality of the metal by having an official mark impressed upon silverware before offering it for sale. In 1379 it was further decreed that "every goldsmith should have his mark by himself." Most of the countries of Europe required that their gold and silverwares be stamped; these marks, from being controlled by the guilds or goldsmiths' halls, are called hallmarks. No such guilds or halls operated in this country. The closest approximation was the Baltimore Assay Office, which operated effectively from 1814 to 1830, where Baltimore silver was assayed, dated and stamped.

Colonial silversmiths marked their silver with their initials, with or without a device in an irregular enclosure which outlined the mark. By the beginning of the nineteenth century the number of silversmiths had increased so that it became necessary to use the full first and last name, often with the middle initial as well. The name of the town was frequently added. At this same time intaglio marks with no enclosures were used. This type of mark was used increasingly throughout the nineteenth century, some of those of the mid- and latter part of the century being retailers' marks. Around 1825, the street address was often added to the full mark. Until the third quarter of the eighteenth century most silversmiths used the letter *I* rather than *J* in their personal name stamps. Roman-type capital letters with serifs were used most often until the middle of the eighteenth century when script letters were employed, especially for full-name marks. Pieces made during partnership in the early days were usually marked with the partners' separate marks. Since the beginning of the nineteenth century, ampersands have been used almost exclusively to indicate partnerships. In addition to the above marks, various pseudo-hallmarks were used, especially between 1825 and the Civil War era. Some were adapted from symbols on state seals or from the Great Seal of the United

States. Other motifs utilized include an eagle, a man's head, a five- or six-point star, an anchor, a lion, and an arm and hammer. Frequently these are accompanied by the letter *C* or *D*. It has been assumed that these letters stand for COIN or DOLLAR; however, the letter *G* occurs about as often as the other two. These markings occur most frequently on silver from the New York area; their meaning, if any, has not been established with certainty.

While the sterling measurement was used, and so marked, in Baltimore from 1800 to 1814, most American silversmiths have used the sterling alloy only since mid-nineteenth century, with the actual STERLING mark in general use only after 1857. Early in the nineteenth century the word COIN began to appear on American silver. PURE COIN was often used in the second quarter of the century and later throughout New England and south to the Carolinas, with the exception of Maryland where the word COIN has not been reported. The mark STANDARD occurs during the same period, mainly on Philadelphia silver. Just which "standard" is not clear. PREMIUM, also used, may mean better than coin.

Date letters, or other dating devices, other than those found on Baltimore silver from 1814 to 1830, were not generally used on American silver until the middle of the nineteenth century when they occurred most frequently on New York silver. These are most often found in a diamond-shaped outline with a number in each of the four corners, similar to the registry marks used on English wares of the same period. Several American firms, in this century, have date-marked their silver. The Gorham Company used letters of the alphabet from 1868 through 1884, at which time a new symbol was adopted for each year until 1933 when they were discontinued. In January, 1941, year markings were resumed on sterling holloware. Reed & Barton dated their holloware from 1928 to 1957 with a different symbol representing each year. The Stieff Company of Baltimore began dating their holloware in 1901. The Tuttle Company silver is marked with a pine tree in a circle and the initials of the incumbent President of the United States. This system began in 1926 when Calvin Coolidge was in office. The Tiffany Company, in 1868, began stamping its silver not only with the company name, but also with the letter *M*, for Edward C. Moore, then its president. Ever since, both the Tiffany name and the initial of the incumbent company president appear on all Tiffany-made silver. The Whiting Manufacturing Company used a series of symbols as year marks from 1905 to 1924. Approximate dating of silver made by some other companies is possible through changes in the firm name or variations in the trademarks used.

With the increase in numbers of large silversmiths' shops employing numerous craftsmen and the rise of actual factories in the 1840s, American silver was marked with the name or device representative of the firm. These trademarks, many of which have been registered in the United States Patent Office, Trademark Division, are the guarantee of quality workmanship and the purity of the silver used. On factory-made goods, wholesalers' or retailers' marks have often been added or used instead of makers' marks, making it difficult to determine the actual maker.

In 1906 the National Stamping Act made it unlawful to indicate by engraved or stamped quality mark, or by label or tag, that the gold or silver content of merchandise was greater than it actually was. In 1961 Congress passed, at the urging of the Jewelers' Vigilance Committee and other industry groups, an amendment designed to pinpoint responsibility for quality marks on gold and silver merchandise. Whoever applies a quality mark to gold or silver merchandise must now stamp a firm name or trademark on the goods in addition to the quality mark. If a trademark is used, that trademark must be registered at the United States Patent Office within thirty days of the goods first being put into interstate commerce or mailed.

Silver obtained by colonial silversmiths from coins or out-of-fashion objects was melted and poured into a mold and allowed to cool and harden. The resulting ingot was then hammered on an anvil until a flat sheet was formed. In order to make a deep, round vessel, the silversmith cut out a circular piece of metal with large shears, having previously prepared a drawing of the vessel he intended to make. Using a compass or scriber, he determined the exact center of the disk and marked it with a punch. The next step was to scribe lightly a series of concentric circles on the disk which served as guidelines in shaping the piece.

First on a wooden block with a shallow circular depression and later on the raising anvil, the flat plate was hammered with even strokes to raise the vessel to the required form. Because hammering makes silver brittle it was necessary to reheat the piece several times on a charcoal forge and then plunge it into a bath of water and sulphuric acid. This reheating, or annealing, toughened or tempered the metal. Further shaping might be done with various tools and anvils. Hammer marks were then removed on a planishing anvil, using special planishing hammers with highly polished surfaces.

Small parts, such as spouts, handles, finials and hinges were cast in molds held in iron frames, called casting flasks. Some handles were raised in two pieces and soldered together. Handles for teapots and coffeepots were carved from wood. Moldings for the rim, base or for decoration were formed by pulling silver strips through a drawing bench with shaped openings in a steel plate. These parts were then soldered to the body.

Several techniques were used for decoration. Embossed designs were hammered into a piece from the inside using an elongated *Z*-shaped instrument called a snarling iron. One end was inserted into the body of the piece and the other end was struck with a hammer. Designs to be engraved or punched onto the surface were done with gravers or chasing punches. For this type of work the vessel was first filled with molten pitch, which hardened and gave protection against the chasing tools penetrating the metal. Small objects might be imbedded in pitch to hold them in place; larger ones were placed on a leather sandbag, Repoussé designs were precisely defined on the outside of the vessel with hammers, punches, and gravers. After the decoration was finished, reheating made the pitch soft enough to be removed.

An immersion in a pickle solution cleaned the surface. The vessel was then burnished, first with a steel and then with a bloodstone burnishing tool. This closed the pores of the metal, compressing them slightly, and left a fine surface sheen impossible to duplicate by mechanical means. After a final polishing, the silversmith struck his mark.

This sketchy account of "raising" a piece of silverware by hand describes a process essentially the same the world over. Such handcraft methods remain basically unchanged and are sometimes used by silversmiths today. Early silversmiths, however, used only these methods. One man, starting with raw materials and only the tools which he used in his own hands, performed all the operations necessary for the creation of a beautiful piece of silver craftsmanship. Inventories of early silversmiths' shops show a surprisingly long list of tools—the basic ones were hammers, punches, anvils and shears. A single silversmith may have had as many as forty or even a hundred hammers. The tools were all *hand* tools, and of prime importance was the ability of the silversmith himself. From the very beginning, the apprenticeship system of England and the Continent prevailed here. At about the age of fourteen a young man was bound to a silversmith by indenture. The master agreed to teach him the "art and mystery" of the craft while providing food, lodging and clothing in return for his labor. Skills were thus passed from one generation to another, often in the same family.

Near the end of the eighteenth century the introduction of rolled sheet silver brought changes to silversmithing. Sheets could be purchased in various thicknesses, thereby eliminating some of the tedious work of earlier days. Though certain forms were still raised up from a single piece of silver, the tendency was to cut out flat pieces of silver to the shape of a pattern, form the metal and solder pieces together in a fraction of the time required for hand raising.

Milling machines which produced stamped silver edgings by the yard were in use at the beginning of the nineteenth century. At the same time, spinning metal against a wooden form or chuck became common. Stamping holloware with ring dies soon became common practice. Previously holloware had to be shaped by successive stampings involving several dies in order to prevent the edges from wrinkling. Then came the sectional chuck from which the core or center piece could be removed so that the entire chuck could be easily removed from the interior of a vessel with a narrow neck.

The introduction of machinery took the silversmith out of the home workshop and into a factory. No longer was the relationship directly between silversmith and patron. A new relationship of manufacturer-wholesaler-retailer-consumer developed, and the silversmith himself often became a specialist in one phase of an in-line factory process.

These changes did not occur all at once, but by 1870 this time-honored craft was almost completely a factory process. Steps in manufacture include stamping, spinning, drawing, casting, polishing, assembling and decorating. In stamping, pull hammers, which operated on the springboard principle, have been replaced by pneumatic drops and by power presses or hydraulic presses. The shaping of a vessel is done by the use of dies made of cast iron, bronze, steel, and more recently, plastics. Frequent annealing is necessary just as in hand raising. In spinning, a disk of silver is fastened between a chuck and a follower. By the application of pressure with a steel spinning tool to the rotating disk, the metal is gradually worked over the chuck or form. Here again, the work is done in stages, with frequent annealings being required as the metal hardens. Chucks were formerly made of wood—preferably dogwood or rock maple. They are now made of steel or nylon. One of the advantages of spinning over stamping or drawing is that the metal can be stretched, or thinned, in one area and packed in another to give added thickness as desired. Drawing is accomplished by the application of pressure on the edges of blanks by means of hold-down rings. Such drawings are often followed by final spinning operations.

Finials, handles, spouts, feet, borders and other "applied" decorations are often cast. These may be cast in sand molds or by the *cire perdue* (lost-wax) process. Sand castings are made by pressing master patterns into a special type of sand which holds the shape impressed into it, even when molten metal is poured into it. Each mold is destroyed in the process of removing the casting, so new molds are constantly needed. The sand, however, can be used again and again. In the lost-wax process, a wax model is embedded in an investment of plaster or clay, the wax melted out and into its place is forced, by centrifugal or other means,

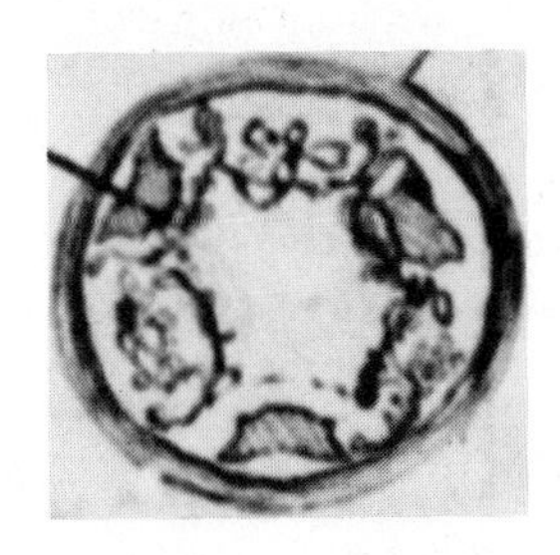

A waiter, chased with scrolls, flowers and fruit, made by Kirk for George Brown in 1848.

Sketch for a crest with a griffin, entered in the Kirk order book for April, 1868.

the molten metal. The wax is lost, and another wax model must be made for every casting.

Assembling involves such operations as filing, fitting, soldering, hammering of seams, flat hammering of waiter bottoms, and applying of mounts. Much of this is still done by hand. A teapot, for instance, may be formed in two halves. These must be soldered with silver solder while held together with soft wire. The resulting seam is then hammered to smooth out rough spots, strengthen the seam and make it invisible. Spout, handle, feet, finial and any decorative mounts are then fitted and soldered into place. Candelabra are made in several sections and assembled, the various parts being put together by crimping in a press. They are later strengthened by a filling of cement or pitch. Candelabra arms are usually made of sterling tubing which must be reinforced with an iron or copper rod for strength and rigidity. Handles are usually cast in two halves which must be soldered together and then soldered to the body of the vessel.

Some of the decorative processes are now accomplished by machine but others are still performed by skilled artisans who have served an apprenticeship of several years. Ornaments such as shields and borders may be cast or stamped and applied. Other designs made from rolled wire are soldered to the body, adding strength as well as decoration. Edge decorations may be cast and soldered on or rolled onto round articles such as plates by passing the edges between two matched hardened steel rolls into which the decoration has been cut.

Decorations to be raised are first "bumped up" from the inside by holding the vessel over the end of a snarling iron. One end of the snarling iron is held in a vise while the other is struck with a hammer. Vibrations from the blows on the snarling iron give the preliminary shaping in the form of bumps raised from the inside. The vessel is then filled with pitch and each part of the design is delicately sculptured from the outside with scores of tools to create the illusion of depth and three-dimensional character. This is chasing, one of the fine arts of silversmithing. Engine turning, as the name implies, is a mechanical process and produces geometric designs on metal surfaces. Piercing, once done only by hand sawing, is now usually done by machine.

Some engraving of letters and monograms can be done with the Hermes engraving machine whose diamond-point cutters work from a model much like a pantograph. Unlike chasing, in which the design is either dented into the metal or raised from the inside, engraving actually cuts away slivers of silver from the surface with sharp gravures or hardened steel tools. Fine lines or bright-cutting may be done, depending on the shape of the tools and the angle at which they are held. Coats of arms, monograms and other designs may be etched into a silver surface by the use of acid and the photoetching process. Oxidizing of highly decorated areas is done by painting or dipping the silver into an acid solution and then removing the solution from the high points and plain surfaces by polishing.

Polishing is done with finely ground pumice on a leather or hard cloth buffing wheel. This is called "sand bobbing." Walrus hide is the best type of leather, as it is available in thicknesses of one inch or more and can be shaped into either flat surfaces or sharp edges. It absorbs the correct amount of sand and oil to give a smooth cutting operation without scratching. Grease buffing follows with cloth buffs and a cutting grease compound which gives a higher polish. The final polishing is imparted by a rouge polish on soft cloth buffs.

There are 149 operations totaling 29 hours of skilled labor involved in the production of a modern decorated coffeepot in a pattern such as *Francis Ist* made by Reed & Barton. Designing of silverware is now done by specially qualified persons, many of them trained in our finest schools of design. Each new design, in the form of sketches, is first submitted to a committee of company officials. These sketches may be revised or modified several times before approval. The design is then sent to the factory and an actual sample made by hand. The exemplar is once again evaluated, not only for its beauty and utility, but also from the standpoint of production requirements and marketing possibilities. Only then is it put into production.

As early as the middle of the seventeenth century, there was a demand for the silversmith and his wares in the urban center of Boston and only slightly later in New York and Philadelphia. Not all early colonists came to this New World in search of religious freedom; some came seeking monetary goals. In this aim, many were immediately successful and lived well, thus requiring luxuries such as beautiful silver for their homes and churches.

Colonial silversmiths of the seventeenth century modeled their wares after Puritan and Restoration styles in England. But, early American silversmiths, while accepting the actual shapes, almost invariably refrained from repeating the elaborate ornamentation found on some seventeenth- and eighteenth-century English silver. These English styles had been affected somewhat by Continental influence through Dutch publications and by immigrant Huguenot silversmiths. Boston silver followed London traditions. Some Philadelphia silver adhered strictly to English forms while other pieces, though English inspired, were modified through the Quaker desire for simplicity. New York silver showed some direct Continental influence because of the presence of Dutch settlers and Huguenot refugees, but here, too, England was the primary design source. The economy of the South, based on large farms and plantations, did not encourage the development of large cities which could support native silversmiths. The South was oriented toward England whence much of their silver was ordered, though the practice did not completely exclude the work of a number of local silversmiths.

During the last decade of the seventeenth century silver styling gradually shifted to the elaborate Baroque style which was exemplified by bold lines, three-dimensional details, fluting, gadrooning, cut-card bands and cast ornament.

By about 1720, Queen Anne styles prevailed—in which emphasis was placed on the inherent beauty of the silver itself, on plain surfaces and on the sinuous Hogarthian "line of beauty" with its curves and reverse curves. From mid-century until the Revolutionary War much elaborate surface ornamentation was applied to the sinuous forms that had appeared a few years earlier. Rococo decoration included not only basic shell motifs, but other naturalistic motifs such as flowers and leaves. The pear shape, so popular a few years earlier, was now inverted.

Classical styles in American silver from 1775 to 1810 were derived largely from English models inspired by the work of Robert Adam. The new republic was being compared to that of ancient Rome, from which Adam drew inspiration. Hence, there was immediate acceptance of the new style in this country. The urn shape was one of its basic elements; decoration featured bands of applied ornament, galleried rims, bright-cutting, swags, wreaths and pendant medallions. Tea services, formerly acquired piece by piece, began to be ordered all to one design.

With the beginnings of industrialization rolling machines made flat sheets of silver readily available. New designs were created by cutting rectangular sections from these sheets, which were then curled into a circle or oval and seamed. Tops and bases were cut to shape and soldered to the body. As the eighteenth century ended, the machine and its capabilities often determined the design of silver.

About 1810 the Empire style was introduced. It was based on Greek and Roman objects unearthed at Herculaneum and Pompeii and on Egyptian antiquities popularized by Napoleon's Egyptian campaign. Empire ornamentation included naturalistic grape vines, cast dolphins, swans, winged lions, undulating snakes, acanthus and laurel leaf motifs, human masks, cast spread eagles and square plinths supported by animal feet. Monumental presentation pieces were made to reward the American heroes of the War of 1812. The Warwick Vase, found in 1770 among the ruins of Hadrian's Villa at Tivoli near Rome, was a favorite model. Small factories were established at this time to make silver articles, mainly tea and dinner services.

Much of the silver of the early Victorian period was overburdened with ornamentation. There was evidence of a Rococo revival before 1840 and by 1850 it was in full swing. This revival lasted well into the 1860s. Rococo curved lines were often exaggerated and decoration was applied with more enthusiasm than taste. Naturalistic ornament was added to objects in such profusion that often the original shape was obscured. While Rococo designs were the most popular, other modes were not excluded; Gothic and Elizabethan strapwork were also used. A Renaissance revival, evident in silver exhibited at the London Crystal Palace in 1851, quickly found its way to this country and remained fashionable until about 1880. Interest in classical urn shapes was revived, but there were straight-sided vessels, too, often with angular handles. Water pitchers, claret jugs and coffeepots were sometimes modeled after the Greek *oenochoe*, or wine pitcher, with trefoil-shaped mouth. There were also globular coffeepots with long cylindrical necks. Borders of gadrooning, beading, Greek key, guilloche and heavy moldings were used. Decorative bands adapted from Greek and Roman friezes were applied to all sorts of vessels. Supports were dolphins, lions, sphinxes, animal paws and elaborately scrolled acanthus leaves. Goat heads, swans, lions, oxen and winged cupids were among the objects cast as finials and used to decorate handles and spouts. Medallions, derived from design books in which cameos of Greece and Rome were illustrated, were a favorite Renaissance motif. Surface ornament was often lacy engraving or all-over repoussé with a matte ground whose dull surface offered a striking contrast to the usual brilliant finish.

From about 1870 until after the turn of the century, American silver was subject to a bewildering welter of styles. There were revivals of French and Italian Renaissance, with Elizabethan, Egyptian, Persian, Jacobean, Japanese, Etruscan and Moorish motifs, often in inharmonious combination. Tea sets of the 1870s are easily identified by the "long-legged" look, angular handles and ornamentations which often bore no relationship to each other or to the shape of the pots themselves. Tea services of the 1880s exhibited a trend away from the long-legged vessels of the earlier decade to a squat shape; some pieces rested on a low rim. The exotic look of Turkish and Persian design was adopted for some long-necked after-dinner coffee services.

The Art Nouveau movement had its beginnings in Europe in the 1880s but did not reach silversmithing in this country until close to the turn of the century, when William Christmas Codman was brought here from England by the Gorham Company to train a select corps of their silversmiths in the new technique. Entirely hand-wrought, Gorham Art Nouveau silver was sold under the names Martelé and Athenic. Art Nouveau in feeling, the Athenic was of Grecian inspiration and combined copper and other metals with silver. The first of these wares was placed on the market in about 1900. Art Nouveau was an attempt to break away from the fetters and concepts of previous historic styles and to bring the fine arts and the crafts into an overall esthetic unity. It is easily identified by its free-flowing organic lines defining sinuous stems, blossoms and leaves. The female form, usually swathed in flowing draperies merging with long flowing hair, is a dominant motif.

Expositions have reflected not only current styles, but have in turn, asserted their influence on further developments. Following the Centennial Exposition, held in Philadelphia in 1876, there was a brief revival of interest in designs of colonial inspiration. This was reflected again in a nationwide interest in colonial styles which was aroused by the Hudson-Fulton Celebration, held in New York in 1909.

The *manufacture* of silverware in the United States dates from the 1840s. Prior to that, there were no regular factories producing plate in this country. The few silversmiths who had opened shops repaired watches, and made cups, snuff boxes, watch chains and other small articles. Several factors were responsible for the industry's rapid mid-century growth. Industrialization and the availability of machinery to perform what had previously been tedious hand labor clearly played a role. So, too, did the discovery of rich silver deposits in North America. Of equal importance was the passage of a protective tariff. In 1842 a number of silversmiths from New York and other cities got together to discuss their trade. A delegation was sent to Washington to meet with Henry Clay, who was supporting protection for American industry. The tariff act, passed in August of that year, levied a duty of 30 per cent on all importations of gold and silverware, whether solid or plated. Nearly all the existing shops enlarged their business immediately after the law was passed.

Few of the silver manufacturing establishments sprang up full grown overnight; most were built up gradually on the growth and death of earlier concerns. Each company has laid a foundation for those that follow and each has touched many others. The growth of Reed & Barton will serve as an example. It began as Babbitt & Crossman, in 1824, to manufacture britannia ware, founded by a jeweler, William Crossman, and that experimenter-in-metals, Isaac Babbitt. The company fortunes and name underwent various changes, Babbitt, Crossman & Company; Crossman, West & Leonard; Taunton Britannia Manufacturing Company; Leonard, Reed & Barton; until finally, in 1840, it emerged in its present form as Reed & Barton.

In 1928 Reed & Barton purchased the Dominick & Haff Company whose history can be traced back to William Gale & Son, silversmiths in New York in 1821, and whose succession of firm names was Gale & North; Gale, North & Dominick; and finally in 1873, Dominick & Haff. William Gale had been an apprentice of Peter & John Targee, silversmiths in New York (John Targee, w. 1797–1841; Peter Targee, w. 1809–1811; together, 1809–1816), who had succeeded to the business of John Vernon, New York silversmith (w. 1787–1816). In 1879 Dominick & Haff purchased from Adams & Shaw (which had been founded about 1873 by Caleb Cushing Adams, for eighteen years the general manager of the Gorham Company, and Thomas Shaw, an Englishman employed by the Gorham Company, until in connection with Tiffany & Company, he formed the manufacturing firm of Thomas Shaw & Company) the tools, fixtures, and patterns that related to the manufacture of silverware (the rest went to the Whiting Manufacturing Company), and which Adams & Shaw had previously purchased from John R. Wendt & Company, of New York.

Reed & Barton, in 1950, added the Webster Company as a subsidiary. It had been founded by George K. Webster in 1869 under the name G. K. Webster & Company. In October, 1958, the Webster Company purchased the Frank W. Smith Silver Company. Frank W. Smith, son of Dr. William A. and Susan F. (Durgin) Smith, entered the employ of his relative, Wm.

B. Durgin (who had been apprenticed to Newell Harding), silversmith of Concord, New Hampshire. He remained with Durgin until the 1880s, when the Smith family moved to Gardner, Massachusetts, and he established his own business. While both the Webster Company and Frank W. Smith Silver Company are divisions of Reed & Barton, they continue to operate independently.

The history of Reed & Barton illustrates the twin roots of the American silverware industry. Some firms, like the parent company, began as britannia makers and then moved into the production of silverplate. Reed & Barton did not begin to manufacture sterling silver until 1889. Others, like its acquisition, Dominick & Haff, were founded by silversmiths and jewelers.

Many of the Connecticut manufacturers started with the production of britannia. Wallace Silversmiths was founded by Robert Wallace in 1833 in an old grist mill where he made britannia spoons. German silver spoons were added about a year later, and in 1875 the production of sterling spoons and forks was begun. The firm did not make sterling holloware until 1891. The International Silver Company was formed in 1898 though the merger of a number of independent New England silversmiths. Of 35 companies which then, or later, became part of International, only the Derby Silver Company; Maltby, Stevens & Curtiss Company; Wm. Rogers Manufacturing Company; Watrous Manufacturing Company; and Wilcox & Evertsen made sterling silver holloware prior to the merger.

Among the companies founded by jewelers are Unger Bros., established in 1870 as Unger & Keen, and The Tiffany Company, founded in 1837, which did not begin to manufacture silver until 1868 when it acquired the silverware factory of Edward C. Moore. The Gorham Company was also founded by a jeweler, Jabez Gorham. It was not until Henry L. Webster joined the firm, in 1831, that the manufacture of silver spoons was begun. In the next decade small articles like thimbles and combs and an occasional napkin ring or fork were produced. The Gorham Company eventually became the largest maker of solid silverware in the world.

Several companies, founded late in the nineteenth century or early in the twentieth, were formed solely for the purpose of producing sterling silver. R. Blackinton, founded in 1862 by Walter Ballou and Roswell Blackinton, makes only sterling silver. The Manchester Silver Company was founded in 1887 by William H. Manchester and has always marketed its wares under the slogan, "If it's Manchester, it's Sterling." The Old Newbury Crafters, incorporated in 1916 by silversmiths of long experience, and Tuttle Silversmiths, begun by Boston silversmith Timothy Tuttle, also make only sterling silver.

Other companies, which began with the production of sterling silver, have, in recent years, expanded into the manufacture of silverplated wares and pewter. Two of these are Lunt Silversmiths and Towle Silversmiths, both of whom can trace their beginning to the pioneer colonial silversmith William Moulton II, whose first silver shoebuckles appeared about 1690. Kirk Silversmiths, founded in 1815 by Samuel Kirk, made only solid silver until late in 1972 when they began the production of a few articles in silverplate. The Stieff Company was founded in 1892 as the Baltimore Sterling Silver Company. Their products were all of sterling silver until they recently began to make lines of reproductions for Williamsburg, Historic Newport and Old Sturbridge Village, some of which are pewter and some silverplate.

Early silversmiths engaged almost entirely in "bespoke" or special order work. The customer's order, sometimes accompanied by a small sketch and the date for which the finished work was promised, was entered in the silversmith's journal. This remained a common practice, at least for sterling holloware, until just before World War I. A few silver companies still accept custom orders today. Customers learned of a silversmith's work through word of mouth and through advertisements in newspapers and periodicals. In 1726, Benjamin Franklin conceived the idea of the introduction of small illustrations in his newspaper, *The Pennsylvania Gazette.* These were one and one-half inch stock cuts of sailing vessels, engraved on wood, which were inserted in the announcements of shipping arrivals and departures. Later, single-column cuts for special advertisers were made.

Advertising received even more prominence in the city directories, the first of which was published in Philadelphia in 1794. In 1818 the first advertising pages with accompanying illustrations appeared. These were used in *Paxton's Philadelphia Annual Advertiser*(sic), which contained 67 full-page ads. These, too, were woodcuts which for many years were the principal medium by which advertising illumination was conveyed in print. Wood engraving fitted in perfectly with the average printer's requirements and, with the advent of stereotyping, could be duplicated and cast in metal in unlimited quantities. The directories' success led to a new type of series, the first of which was published in New York in 1853 as *The Illustrated American Biography.* The publishers were quick to point out that, "Alternating, as they do, with the portraits and biographies, every advertisement comes directly under the eye of the reader. . . ." Silversmiths also advertised in such popular nineteenth-century pictorials as *Gleason's Pictorial Drawing-Room Companion, Harper's Weekly, Leslie's Weekly* and *Godey's Lady's Book.* Later they advertised to retailers in such trade publications as *The Jeweler's Circular.*

Silver manufacturers also received publicity from the public display of their wares. They presented their dazzling displays at international expositions, beginning with the first one in London in 1851. Presentation pieces, prominent among the early items made in solid silver, were also often publicly displayed and received much notice thereby. These were awarded to war heroes, prominent political figures and others. Trophies were awarded for horse-racing and yachting. The launching of every battleship and cruiser was the occasion for the presentation of an elaborate service. This silver was often ornate and extreme in style and constituted one of the major products of American silver manufacturers. Laden with symbolic emblems and motifs appropriate for the occasion, or the place represented, each piece was created specially for a particular occasion and therefore is rarely represented in a manufacturer's catalog.

Catalogs for solid silver were, in fact, not issued until late in the nineteenth century. The manufacturers of silverplate, on the other hand, began issuing elaborate, illustrated catalogs of their wares soon after the Civil War. The rapid development of lithography after the war, the perfection of electrotypography, which made possible large-scale application of relatively inexpensive wood engravings, and improved printing presses brought together all the elements necessary for the production of such catalogs. The makers of britannia wares, who had early learned the advantages of wholesale distribution, were quick to adapt their marketing skills to silverplate. The workers in precious metals followed the tradition of special orders placed through their own small shops or through jewelers. Furthermore, large-scale production of sterling holloware for domestic use developed relatively late. Not until the 1870s was sufficient bullion available at a price which enabled manufacturers to produce articles the middle classes could afford. Sterling holloware catalogs, therefore, were published later and were never issued with as much frequency as those for silverplate.

Suggestions for further reading

AMERICAN HERITAGE HISTORY OF AMERICAN ANTIQUES FROM THE REVOLUTION TO THE CIVIL WAR. Edited by Marshall B. Davidson. New York: American Heritage Pub. Co., Inc., 1968.

AMERICAN HERITAGE HISTORY OF ANTIQUES FROM THE CIVIL WAR TO WORLD WAR I. Edited by Marshall B. Davidson. New York: American Heritage Pub. Co., Inc., 1969.

ANTIQUES, *The Magazine*. New York, 1922-

CURRIER, ERNEST M. *Marks of Early American Silversmiths.* Portland, Maine: Southworth-Anthoensen Press, 1938. Reprinted 1970 by Robert Alan Green, Harrison, New York.

ENSKO, STEPHEN G. C. *American Silversmiths and Their Marks, III.* Privately printed, 1948.

FALES, MARTHA GANDY. *Early American Silver for the Cautious Collector.* New York: Funk & Wagnalls, 1970.

HOOD, GRAHAM. *American Silver, A History of Style.* New York: Praeger Publishers, 1971.

THE KIRK COLLECTOR. Baltimore, 1972-

MCCLINTON, KATHERINE MORRISON. *Collecting American 19th Century Silver.* New York: Charles Scribner's Sons, 1968.

19TH-CENTURY AMERICA, *Furniture and other Decorative Arts.* Introduction by Berry B. Tracy. New York: Metropolitan Museum of Art, 1970.

RAINWATER, DOROTHY T. *American Silver Manufacturers.* Hanover, Pennsylvania: Everybody's Press, 1966.

SILVER (formerly SILVER-RAMA). Vancouver, Washington, January 1968-

THE SPINNING WHEEL. Hanover, Pennsylvania, 1945-

Silver collections in American museums

CALIFORNIA Los Angeles County Museum of Art, Los Angeles (Marble Collection); Henry E. Huntington Art Gallery, San Marino (Munro Collection)

CONNECTICUT Connecticut Historical Society, Hartford, Wadsworth Atheneum, Hartford (Hammerslough Collection); Yale University Art Gallery, New Haven (Garvan and Phillips collections); Society of the Founders of Norwich, Conn., Norwich (Joseph Carpenter Shop)

DELAWARE Delaware State Museum, Dover (Delaware makers); The Henry Francis du Pont Winterthur Museum, Winterthur; The Historical Society of Delaware, Wilmington

DISTRICT OF COLUMBIA Daughters of the American Revolution Museum; Museum of History and Technology, Smithsonian Institution

ILLINOIS Art Institute of Chicago, Chicago

MARYLAND U. S. Naval Academy Museum, Annapolis (silver with naval historical associations); The Baltimore Museum of Art, Baltimore (Baltimore, Annapolis and Eastern Shore silversmiths represented); Maryland Historical Society, Baltimore (Maryland silversmiths); The Peale Museum, Baltimore (Kirk Collection)

MASSACHUSETTS Addison Gallery of American Art, Phillips Academy, Andover; Museum of Fine Arts, Boston (Boston and other New England silversmiths. Permanent exhibit of the work of Paul Revere, his portrait and tools); Fogg Art Museum, Cambridge; The Heritage Foundation Collection, Old Deerfield (also demonstration of silversmithing); Museum of the American China Trade, Milton (China Trade silver); Sterling and Francine Clark Art Institute, Williamstown: Worcester Art Museum, Worcester; Towle Silversmiths, Newburyport; Taunton Museum and Genealogical Library, Taunton (Taunton manufacturers)

MICHIGAN The Henry Ford Museum, Dearborn; The Detroit Institute of Arts, Detroit

MINNESOTA The Minneapolis Institute of Arts, Minneapolis

MISSOURI William Rockhill Nelson Gallery of Art, Kansas City; City Art Museum, St. Louis

NEW HAMPSHIRE Currier Gallery of Art, Manchester

NEW YORK The Brooklyn Museum, Brooklyn; Albany Institute of History and Art, Albany (Albany silversmiths); The Metropolitan Museum of Art, New York (American Wing exhibits silver in room settings. Special exhibits. New York craftsmen represented especially. A new area in the American Wing added to house the arts of the 19th and 20th centuries); Museum of the City of New York, New York (New York silversmiths represented especially. Presentation silver); New-York Historical Society, New York (New York silversmiths represented especially. Presentation silver); The Jewish Museum, New York (Judaica); West Point Museum, West Point (silver with U. S. Army associations)

OHIO Cincinnati Art Museum, Cincinnati; Cleveland Museum of Art, Cleveland

OREGON The Portland Art Museum, Portland (Nunn Collection)

PENNSYLVANIA The Historical Society of Pennsylvania, Philadelphia; Philadelphia Museum of Art, Philadelphia (Philadelphia silver especially)

RHODE ISLAND Rhode Island School of Design, Museum of Art, Providence (American silver, especially local)

SOUTH CAROLINA The Charleston Museum, Charleston

TEXAS Museum of Fine Arts, Houston (Bayou Bend Collection)

VIRGINIA Virginia Museum of Fine Arts, Richmond; Colonial Williamsburg, Inc., Williamsburg (demonstrations of silversmithing)

"Battleship silver," designed for presentation to ships named for the various states or for cruisers named after cities, has, in many cases, been "retired from active service" and is on view in state houses, governors' mansions or capitol buildings.

CONDUCTED TOUR: Gorham Mfg. Co., Providence, Rhode Island. 1:30 P.M. Mon. through Thurs.; free; no tours Nov. 15 through Jan. 8 or the first three weeks in July.

GORHAM MANUFACTURING COMPANY, 1888

Jabez Gorham, born February 18, 1792, in Providence, Rhode Island, is credited with founding the Gorham Manufacturing Company. However, it was his son, John Gorham, who developed the small shop, employing ten to twelve workmen, into what eventually became the largest manufacturer of solid silverware in the world.

A mechanical genius, John Gorham quickly recognized the advantages of machinery. Scant progress had been made along this line; the small amount of machinery in the plant was driven by horsepower. Soon after John Gorham assumed leadership of the company, a steam engine was set up and a brick building was erected in the rear of the old shop. He broadened the use of machinery, purchasing whatever was available for his purpose, designing and building other machinery for specific operations.

John Gorham's search for new and better ways to make silverware was not confined to machines. His investigations in Europe convinced him that, while American workmen were equal if not superior in the use of machinery, in manipulation and dexterity and care in hand labor the foreign silversmiths were far in advance of his countrymen. Besides returning with broader personal knowledge himself, he also brought silversmiths skilled in the manufacture of holloware back from England.

The firm made steady progress, and, by 1861, was employing about two hundred workmen and distributing its wares extensively in this country and Canada. It became the Gorham Manufacturing Company in 1863 and was incorporated in 1865. In 1868 Gorham abandoned the coin silver standard and adopted the sterling standard. At the same time the familiar trademark, a lion, an anchor and a capital *G*, was formally adopted for use on all sterling articles, though a variation of this mark had been in use on some pieces as far back as 1848.

The company continued to grow, not only within itself, but by the acquisition of other firms. Silver manufacturers who made sterling hollowares and are now part of the Gorham company are: Whiting Mfg. Co., organized by Albert T. Tifft and Wm. D. Whiting in 1840; Wm. B. Durgin Co., founded in 1853; Alvin Mfg. Co., founded in 1886; Graff, Washbourne & Dunn, established in 1899; Mount Vernon Company Silversmiths, founded in 1903 through the merger of Hayes & McFarland, the Mauser Mfg. Co. and Roger Williams Silver Company; Friedman Silver Co., founded in 1908; and the Quaker Silver Co., founded about 1930.

The Gorham firm has long been a trend-setter. Their 1888 catalog clearly presages styles of the 1890s. In addition to the sterling holloware reproduced here, there were offered: three waiters, four child's sets, twenty-four cups, four hair brushes, one nail brush, two clothes brushes, one hat brush and seven bonbon dishes.

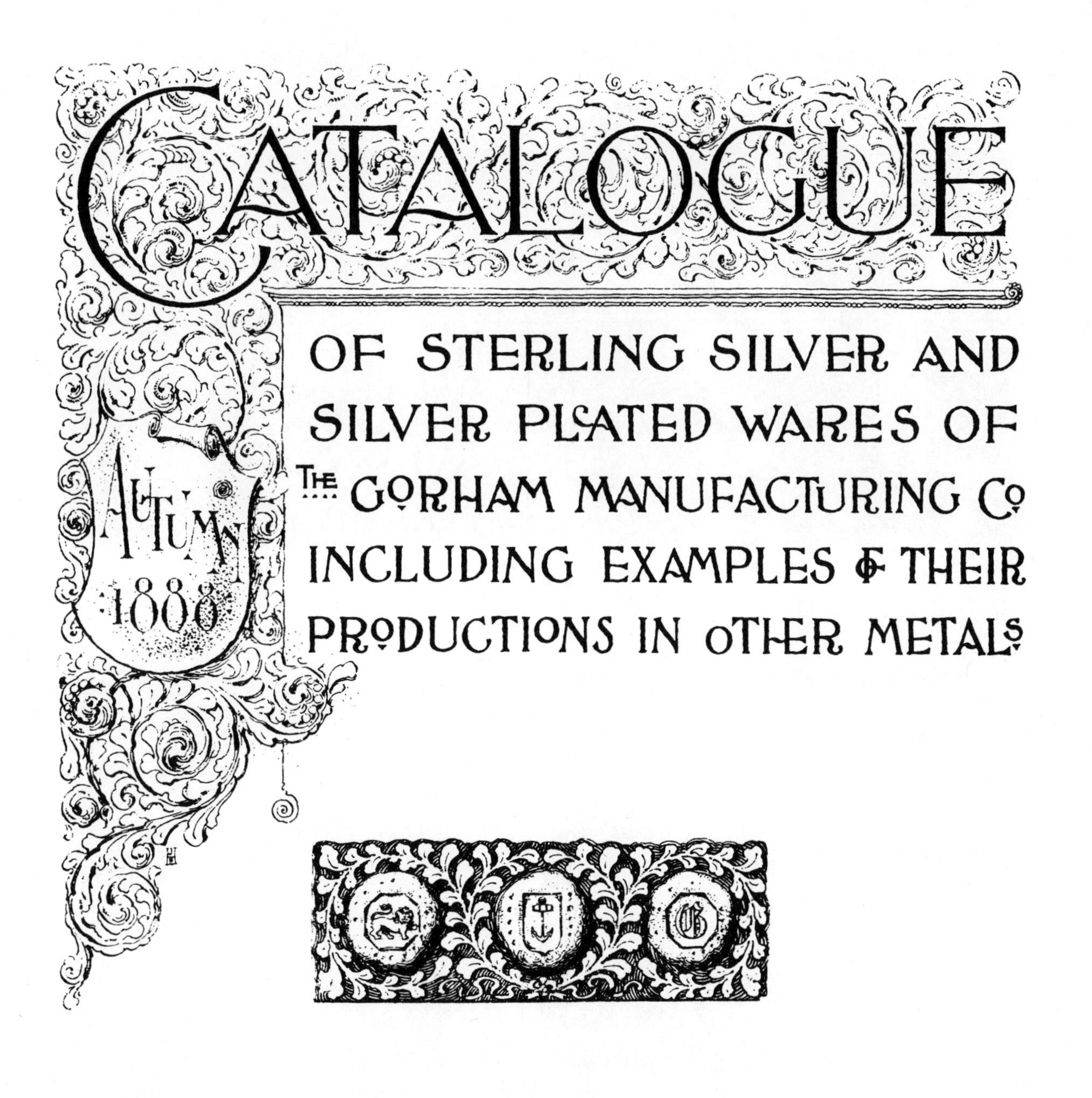

NEW YORK: BROADWAY AND 19TH ST

AND 9 MAIDEN LANE

THE OLD
GORHAM M.F.G. Co
SILVERSMITHS
CATALOGUE
YEAR 1888.
NEW YORK - BROADWAY & 19 STR
9 MAIDEN LANE
CHICAGO - 137 STATE STREET
SAN FRANCISCO - 120 SUTTER · S
MANUFACTORY PROVIDENCE · R · I ·
F.A. HELLER

REPOUSSÉ CHASED

NO. 1930

KETTLE—Height, 12½ in. Capacity, 3½ pints COFFEE—Height, 7½ in. Capacity, 2½ pints TEA—Height, 5½ in. Capacity, 2½ pints

NO. 2100

COFFEE—Height, 9 in. Capacity, 1½ pints TEA—Height, 7 in. Capacity, 1½ pints

NO. 2170

COFFEE—Height, 10 in. Capacity, 2 pints TEA—Height, 8¼ in. Capacity, 2½ pints

NO. 2150

COFFEE—Height, 6½ in. Capacity, 3 pints TEA—Height, 5 in. Capacity, 2½ pints

REPOUSSÉ CHASED

No. 2110

COFFEE—Height, 9 in. Capacity, 3 pints   TEA—Height, 6½ in. Capacity, 2¼ pints

REPOUSSÉ CHASED

No. 2030

KETTLE—Height, 12½ in. Capacity, 3 pints   COFFEE—Height, 8½ in. Capacity, 2 pints   TEA—Height, 7 in. Capacity, 2 pints

STERLING SILVER

No. 2090

KETTLE—Height, 12½ in. Capacity, 2½ pints

COFFEE—Height, 7 in. Capacity, 2½ pints

TEA—Height, 6 in. Capacity, 2 pints

STERLING SILVER

No. 1810

KETTLE—Height, 10½ in. Capacity, 2½ pints

COFFEE—Height, 6 in. Capacity, 2½ pints

TEA—Height, 3½ in. Capacity, 2 pints

	Kettle	Coffee.	Tea
Height	13½ inches.	9 inches.	6 inches.
Capacity	5 pints.		

	Coffee.	Tea
Height	8 inches.	5½ inches.
Capacity	3 pints.	2 pints.

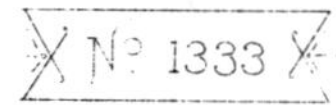

	Kettle	Coffee.	Tea
Height	11½ inches.	7¼ inches.	5 inches
Capacity	4 pints.	3 pints.	2½ pints.

No. 1770

	Kettle	Coffee.	Tea
Height	12½ inches.	6½ inches.	5½ inches.
Capacity	3½ pints.	3 pints.	2½ pints.

Kettle No 2050 Chased

Kettle No 2050. Plain.

No 2050.

	Kettle	Coffee.	Tea
Height	inches.	8 inches.	5½ inches.
Capacity	pints.	2⅞ pints.	2¼ pints.

TETE A TETE SETS.

In 4 Sizes to Match Creamers.
Scale ½ Height

STERLING SILVER PEPPERS & SALTS. GORHAM M'F'G CO.

STERLING SILVER FLASKS. GORHAM M'F'G CO.

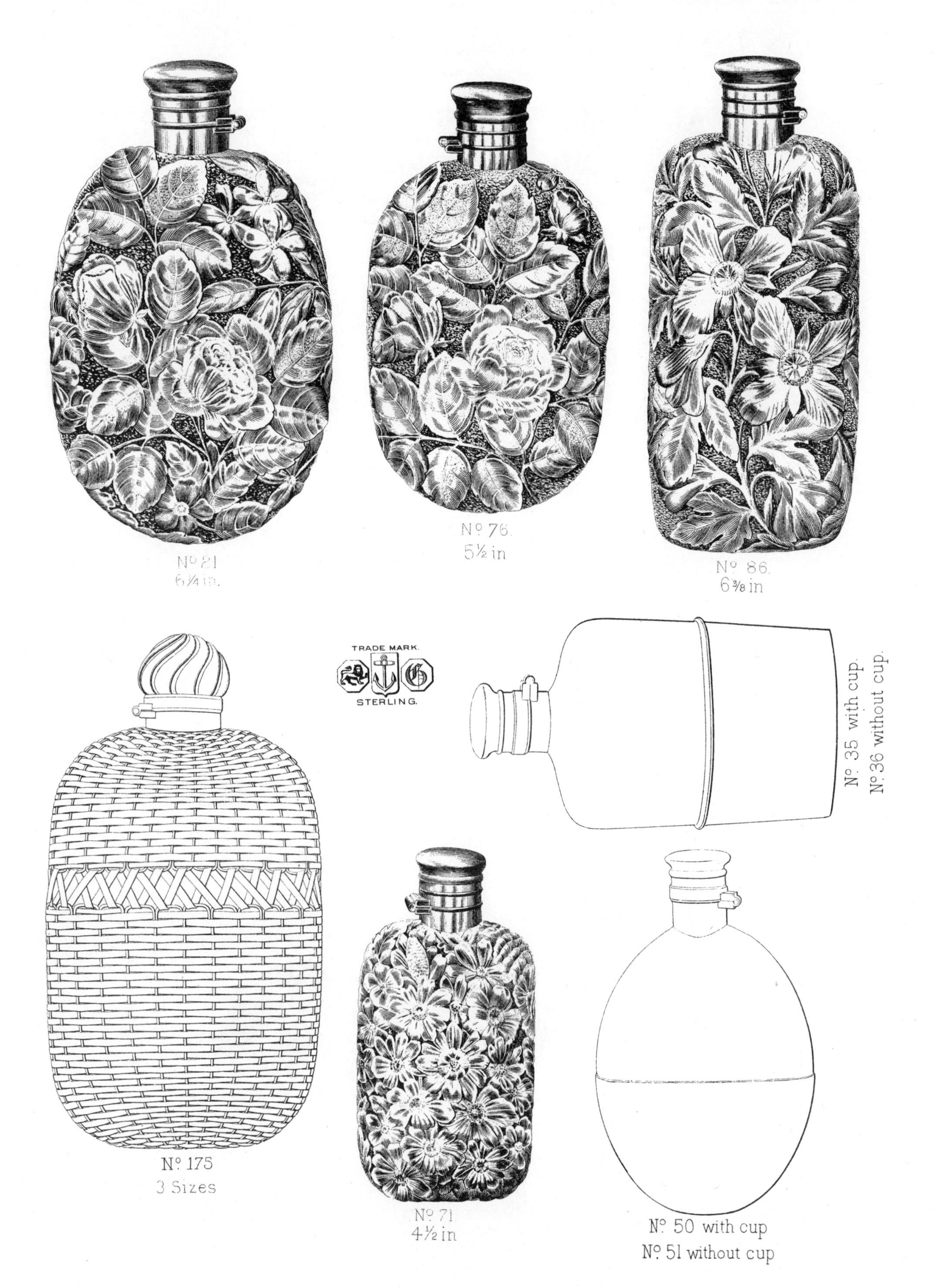

Nº 81
6¼ in.

Nº 76.
5½ in

Nº 86.
6⅜ in

Nº. 35 with cup.
Nº. 36 without cup.

Nº 175
3 Sizes

Nº 71
4½ in

Nº. 50 with cup
Nº. 51 without cup

STERLING SILVER OLIVE DISHES

GORHAM M'F'G CO.

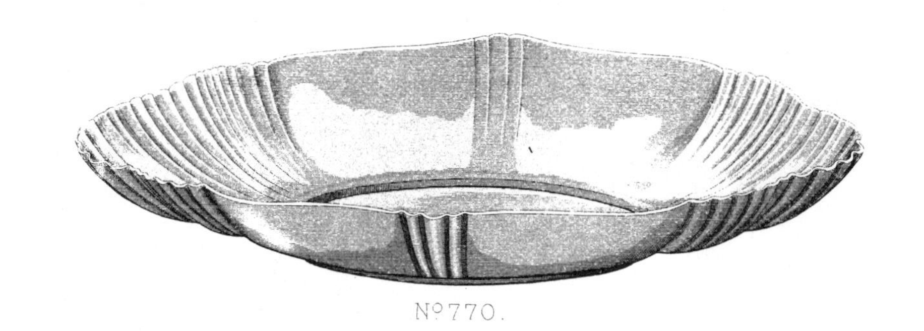

Nº 770.

Nº 775.

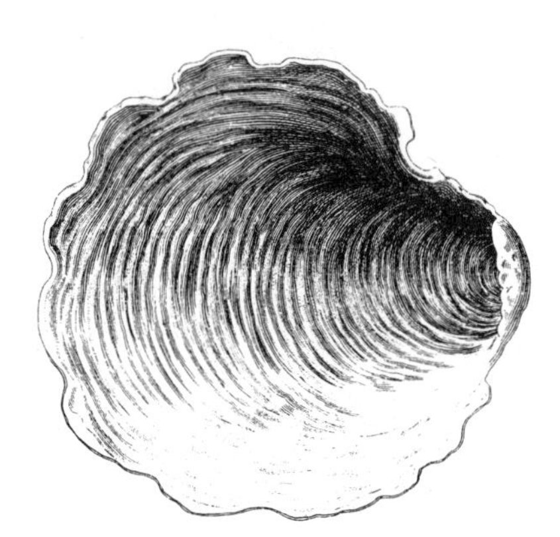

Nº 535

TRADE MARK.

STERLING.

Nº 530.

Nº 525.

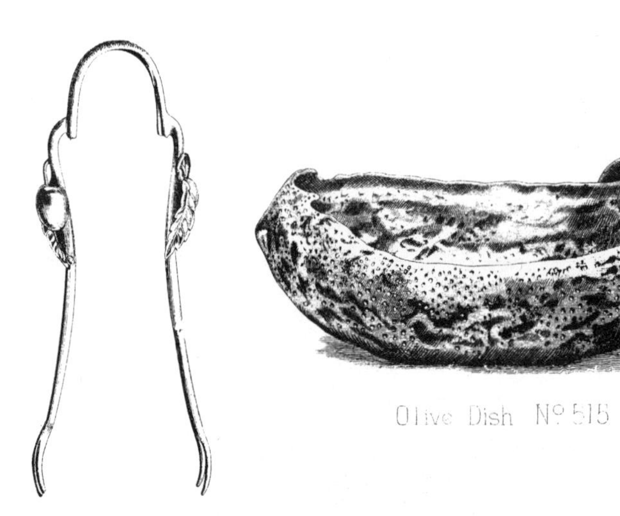

Olive Dish Nº 515

STERLING SILVER PITCHERS. GORHAM M'F'G CO.

No. 1345
Capacity, 4 pints

No 1430
Capacity, 3 pints

No. 1465

Capacity, 2 pints

No. 1415

Capacity, 6 pints

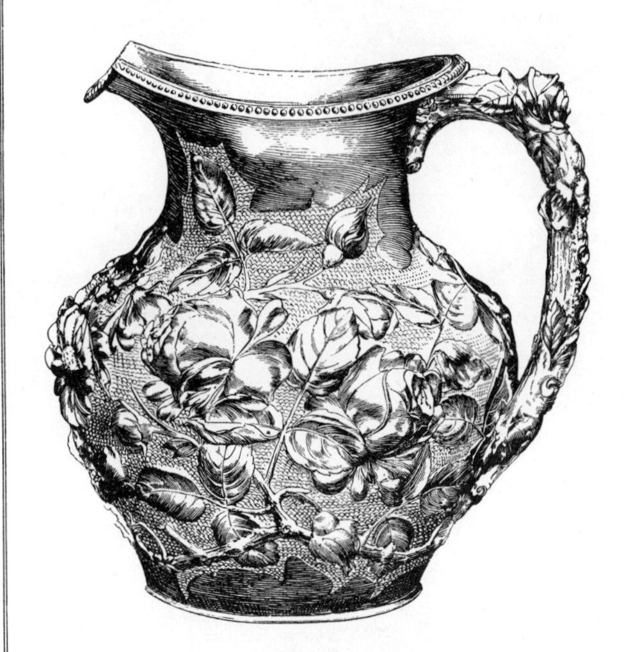

No. 1385
Capacity, 4 pints

No. 1515
Capacity, 4 pints

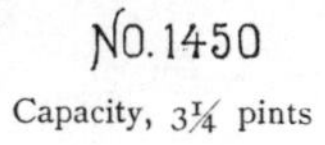

No. 1450
Capacity, 3¼ pints

No. 1505
Capacity, 1½ pints

No. 2175
No. 2905
No. 2905
No. 2510.
No. 2505
No. 2590
BOWLS.
BERRY
No. 2455

N° 2460
N° 2570.
BERRY
BOWLS
N° 2580
N° 2595.

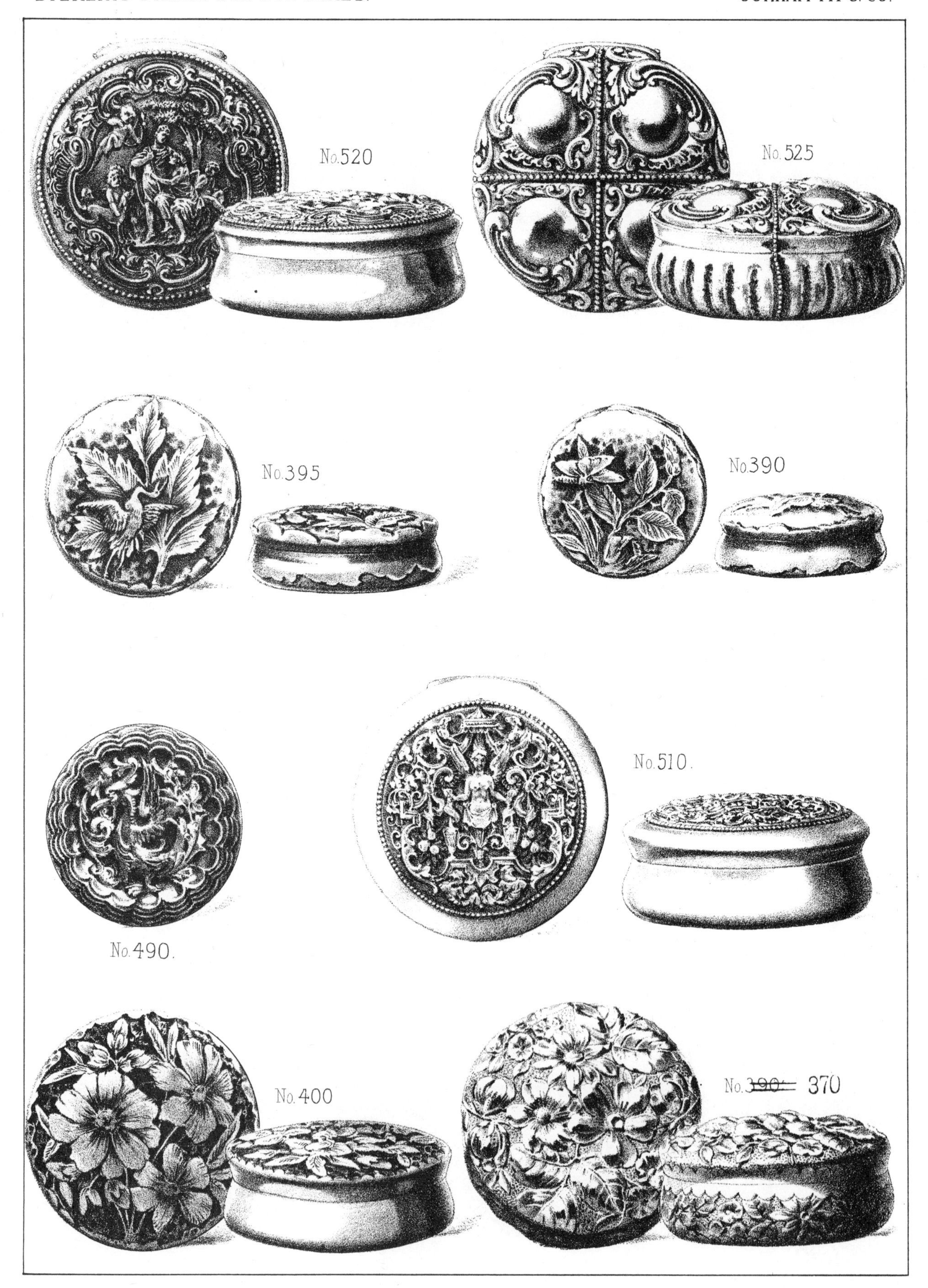
No. 520
No. 525
No. 395
No. 390
No. 510.
No. 490.
No. 400
No. ~~390.~~ 370

No. 3698 (Chased).

No. 3721.

No. 3860.

No. 3930.

No. 3965.

No. 3991.

No. 672.

No. 882.

No. 1150.

No. 1210.

No. 1246.

No. 1300.

No. 1365.

No. 1421.

No. 1422.

No. 1465.

No. 1480.

No. 1522.

STERLING SILVER NAPKIN RINGS. GORHAM M'F'G CO.

No. 1530.

No. 1531.

No. 1545.

No. 1560.

No. 1575.

No. 1595.

No. 1600.

No. 1605.

No. 1655.

No. 1720.

No. 1740.

No. 1760.

No. 1770.

No. 1805.

No. 1810.

No. 1815.

No. 1820.

No. 1860.

No. 1865.

No. ~~1885.~~
1875

No. 1895.

No. 1910.

No. 1915.

No. 1925.

No. 310.

No. 435.

No. 450.

No. 455.

No. 550.

No. 585.

No. 595.

No. 600.

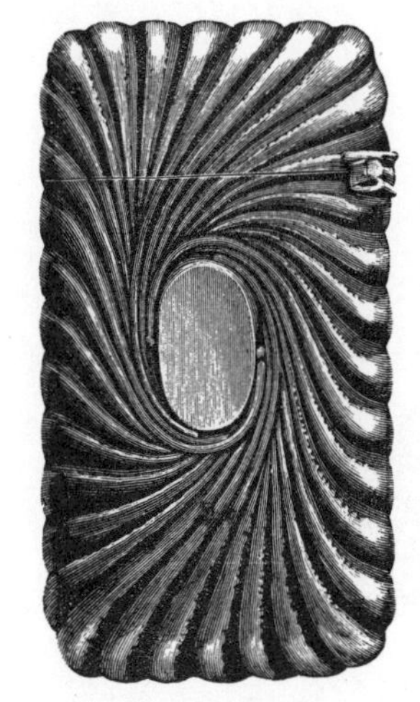

No. 610.

No. 620.

No. 625.

No. 660.

STERLING SILVER MATCH BOXES.

No. 665.

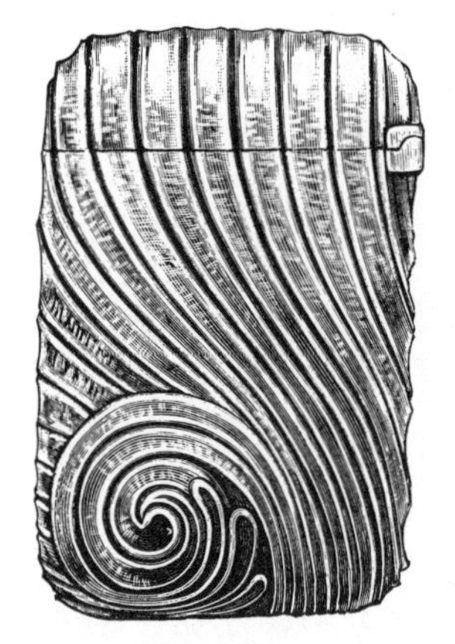

No. 670.

No. 675.

No. 680.

No. 685.

No. 690.

No. 695.

Reverse.

TEA STRAINERS.

No. 23.

No. 24.

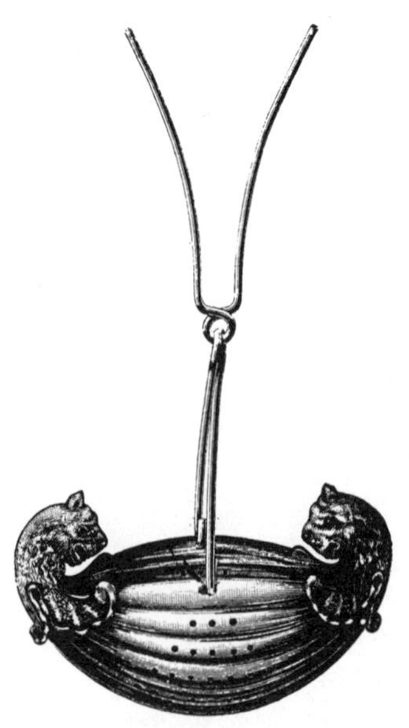

No. 25.

No. 50.

No. 220.

No. 340.

No. 30.

No. 40.

No. 50.

No. 55.

STERLING CIGARETTE AND TOBACCO BOXES. GORHAM M'F'G CO.

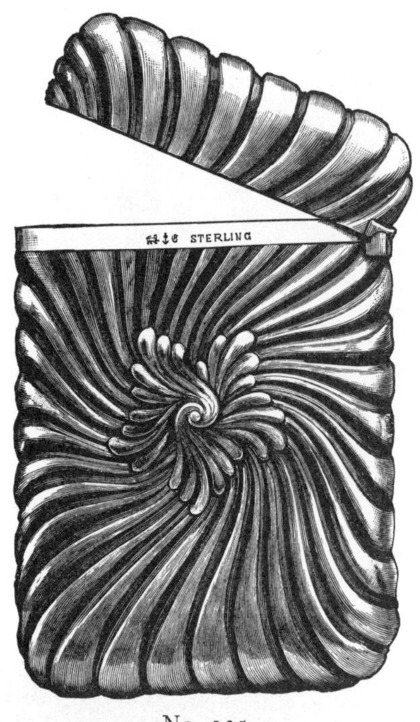

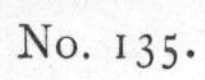

No. 135.

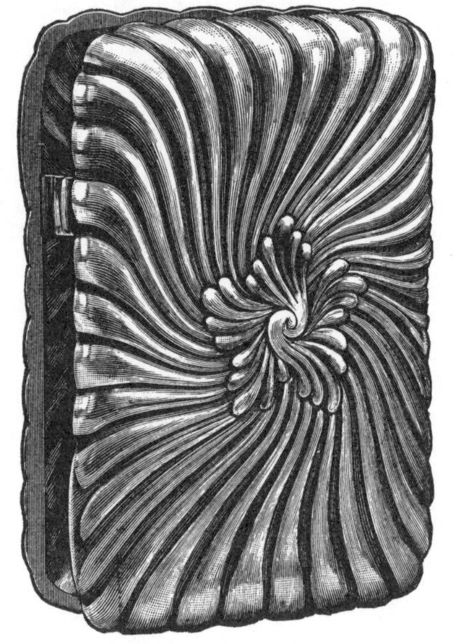

No. 140.

No. 130.

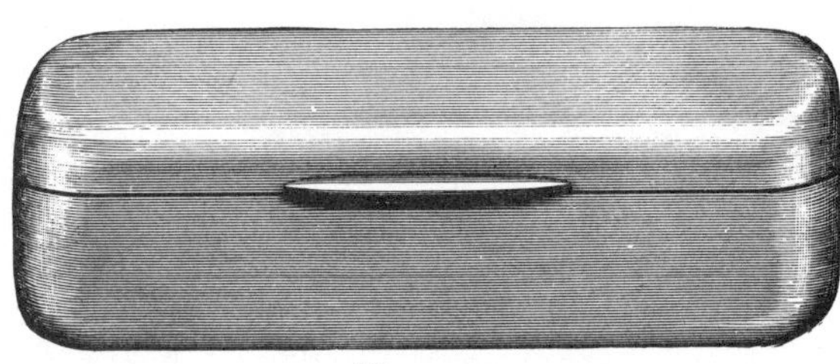

No. 705.

No. 145.

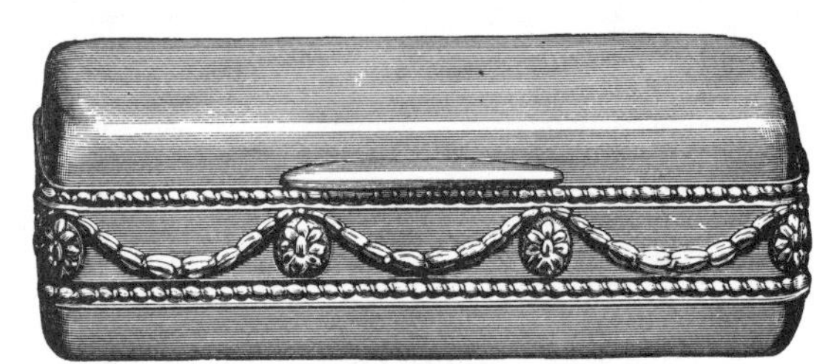

No. 710.

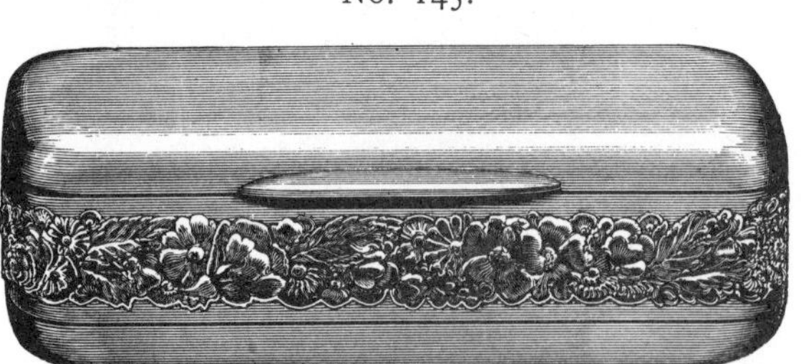

No. 715.

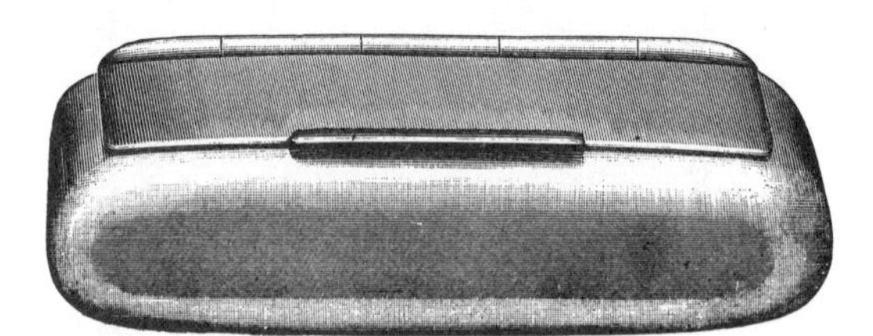

No. 720.

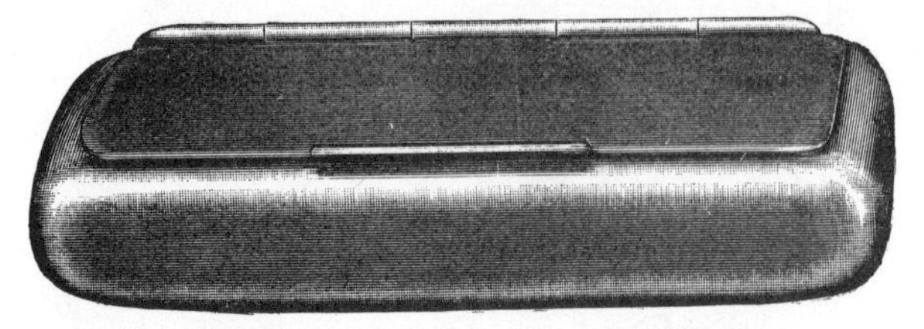

No. 725.

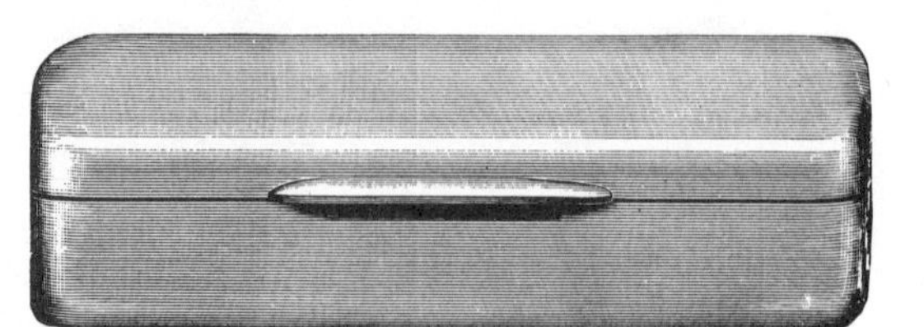

No. 700.

STERLING SILVER BOOK MARKS

GORHAM M'F'G CO.

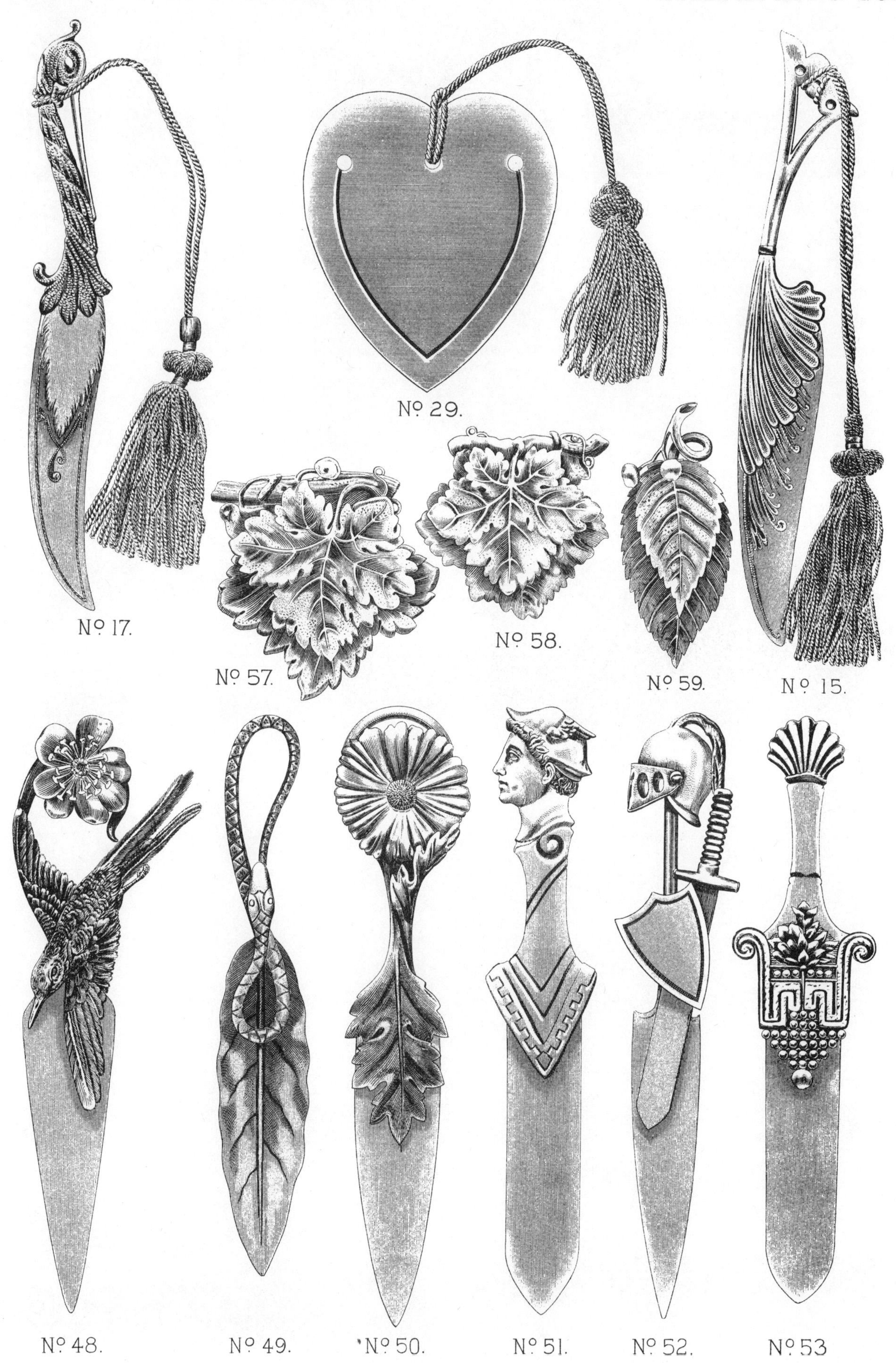

STERLING SILVER BOOK MARKS

GORHAM M'F'G CO.

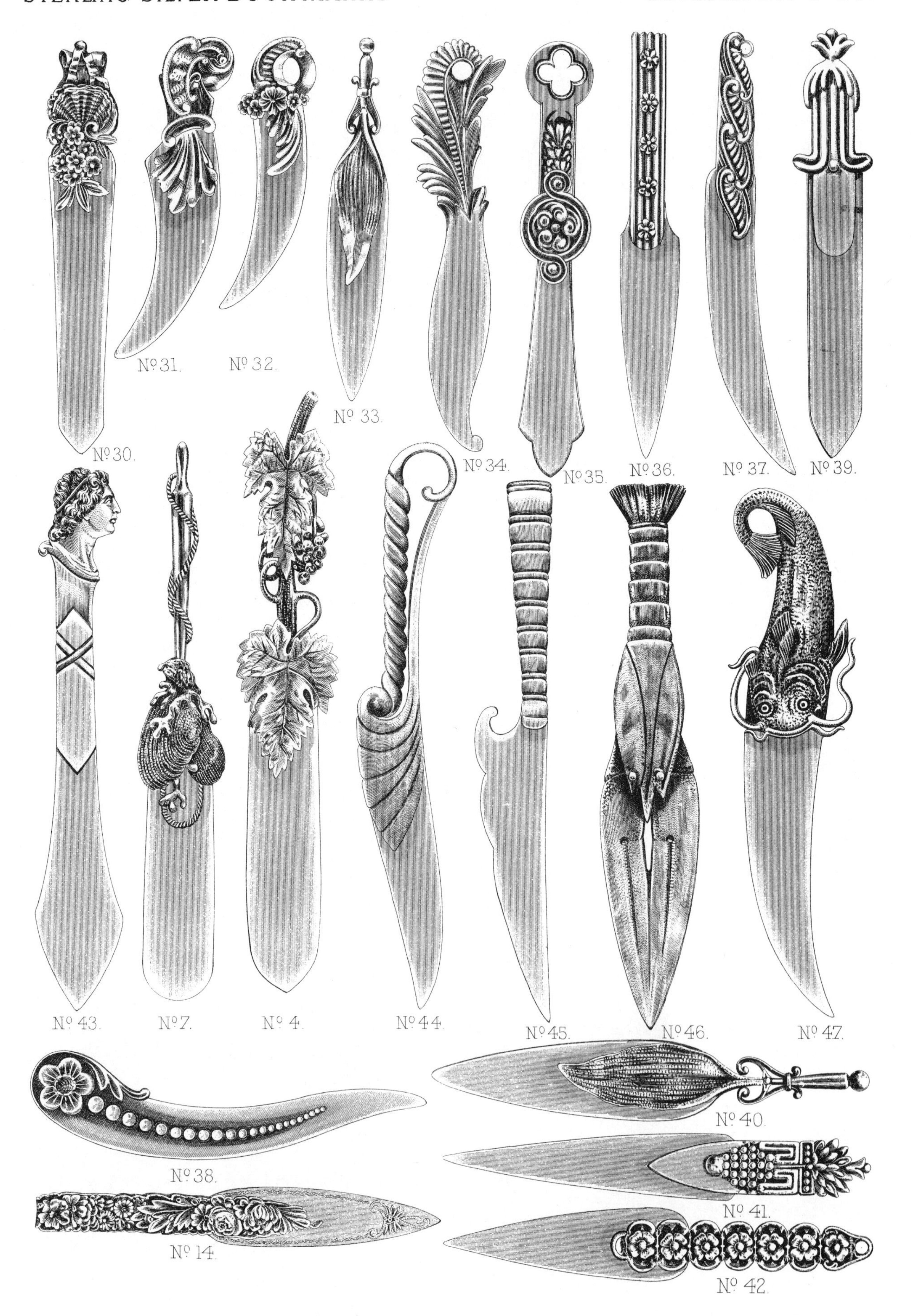

540
542
545
Puff Boxes.
550
345
Puff Boxes and Trays.
16
Mirror.
350
355
Half Length.
165
150
Hair Pin Tray.
Glove Stretcher, Large.
Glove Stretcher, Small
Hair Pin Box.
160
Hair Pin Box.

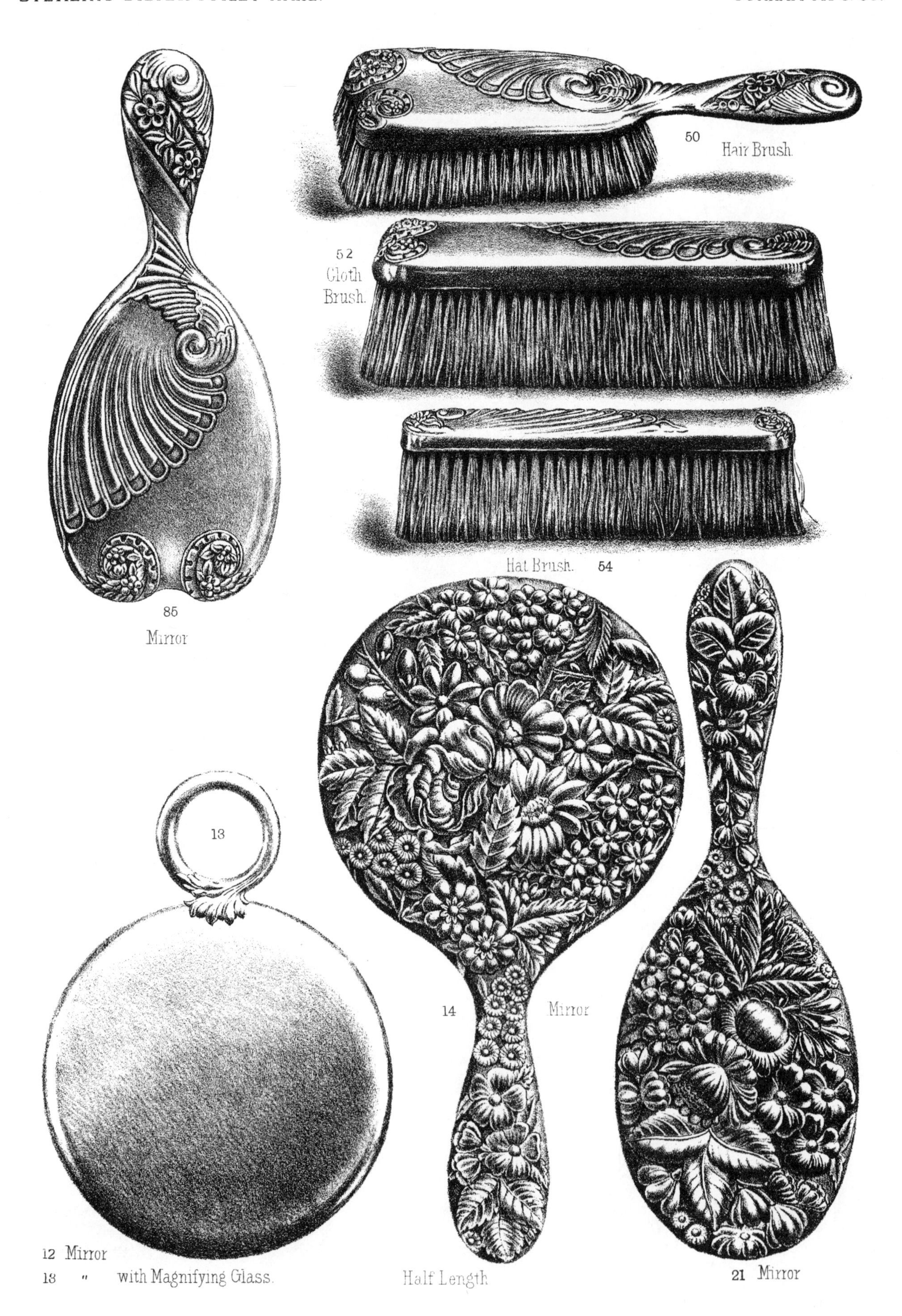
50 Hair Brush.
52 Cloth Brush.
Hat Brush. 54
85 Mirror
13
14 Mirror
12 Mirror
13 " with Magnifying Glass.
Half Length
21 Mirror

63
53
43
35
21
13
5
6
12
Soap Box.
13
Soap Box.
3960
Shaving Cup.
·SILVER·&·SILVER·MOUNTED·
TOILET·GOODS
·GORHAM·M'F'G·C°.·
Half Length.
25
Shaving Brush.
30
Shaving Brush.

446.
Chased

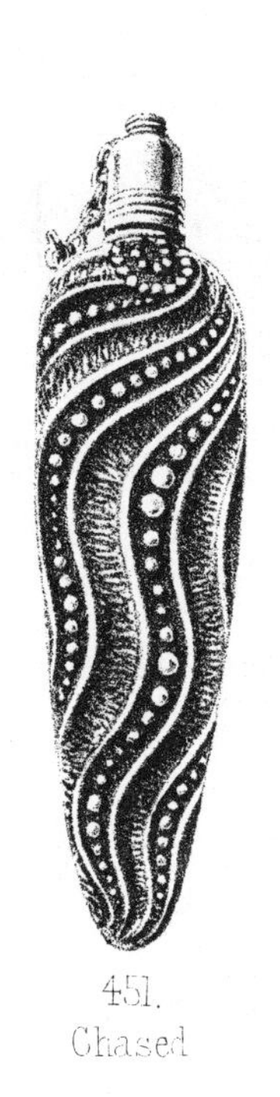

451.
Chased

239.
Etched

230.
Chased

455.
Chased

230.
Etched

456.
Chased

Full Size

GORHAM *MARTELÉ*, 1900

In 1891 William Christmas Codman, English silversmith and designer, was brought to this country to head the design department at Gorham. Four years later he directed an elite corps of their silversmiths in the creation of Art Nouveau designs. These articles were made of .950 fine silver and marketed under the name *Martelé*. All were, as the name implies, wrought from flat sheets of silver solely by the use of the hammer in the hands of a skilled artisan. The marks of the hammer were left upon the surface, giving a soft misty texture which cannot be obtained in any other way. This is a technique in which no piece can be duplicated exactly because no mechanical aids are used. Vases, bowls and tankards were the first articles made, but entire dinner services and ornamental pieces were soon added.

The catalog, from which all the Art Nouveau designs included are reproduced here, was issued in French—evidently for the foreign market—and was distributed by Gorham's Paris representative, Spaulding & Co. The description of each article was printed on a transparent overlay. They are listed below in the order in which they appear.

Service de Toilette, Martelé, "Matin et Soir"
Aiguière Martelé
Bol à Punch martelé, "Les Fleurs"
Aiguière à eau de rose et plateau martelé, "La Vague"
Service à liqueur, verre Favrile et argent martelé
Service tête-à-tête à thé et plateau, jade et or martelé
Coupe d'amour, martelée, emaillée
Coupe d'amour, verre et argent martelé
Carafe à vin de bordeaux, verre et argent martelé, "La Vigne"
Candélabre martelé, "Nuit et Matin"
Service à café, verre et argent martelé
Pièce de centre pour table, dix-huitième siècle
Calice argent martelé avec bassin en or orné de pierreries et émaillé et Patène en or avec plaque en argent émaillé

The

GORHAM

Manufacturing Co.

ORFÈVRES

NEW YORK

Representée à Paris par

SPAULDING & CO.

36 Avenue de l'Opéra

NEW YORK

MCM

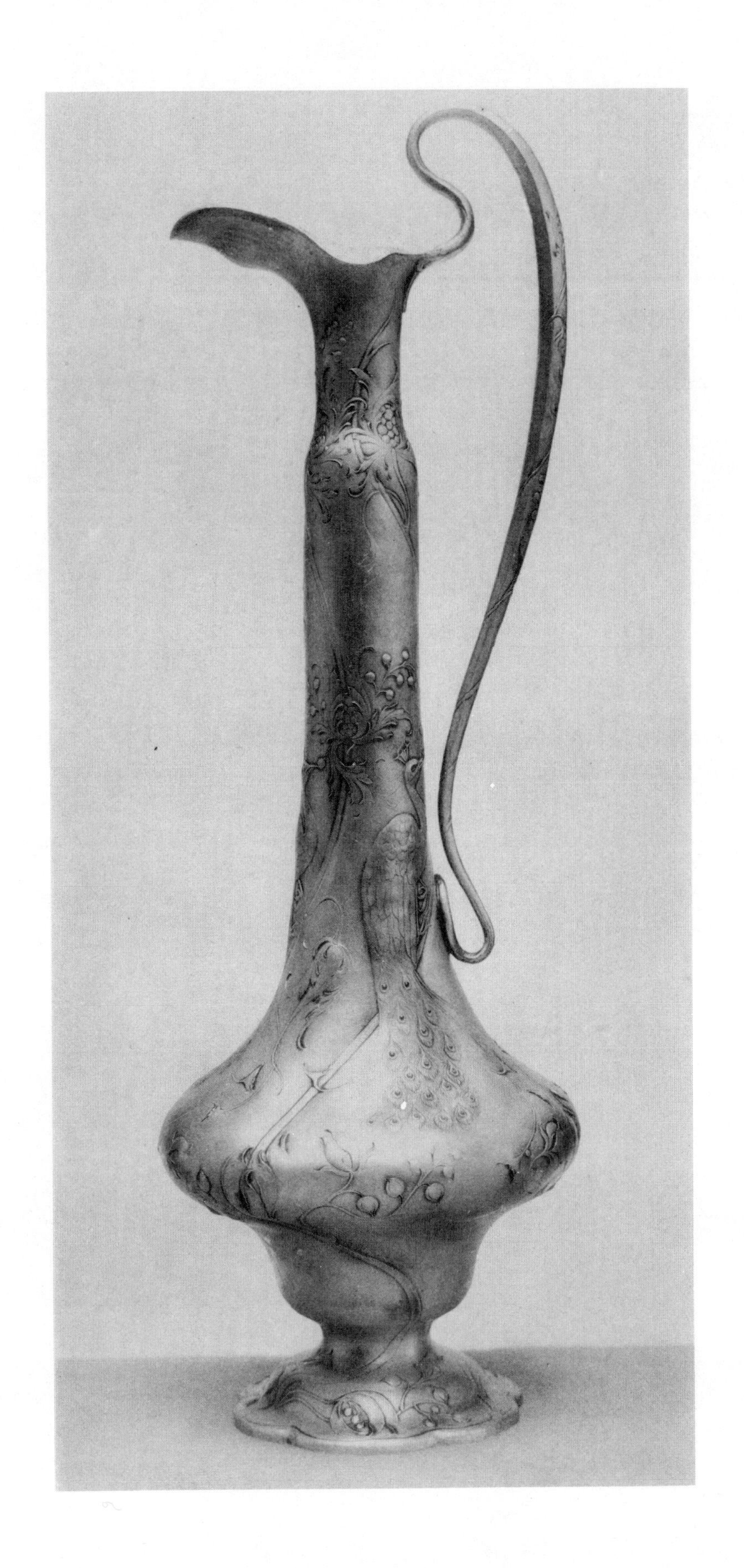

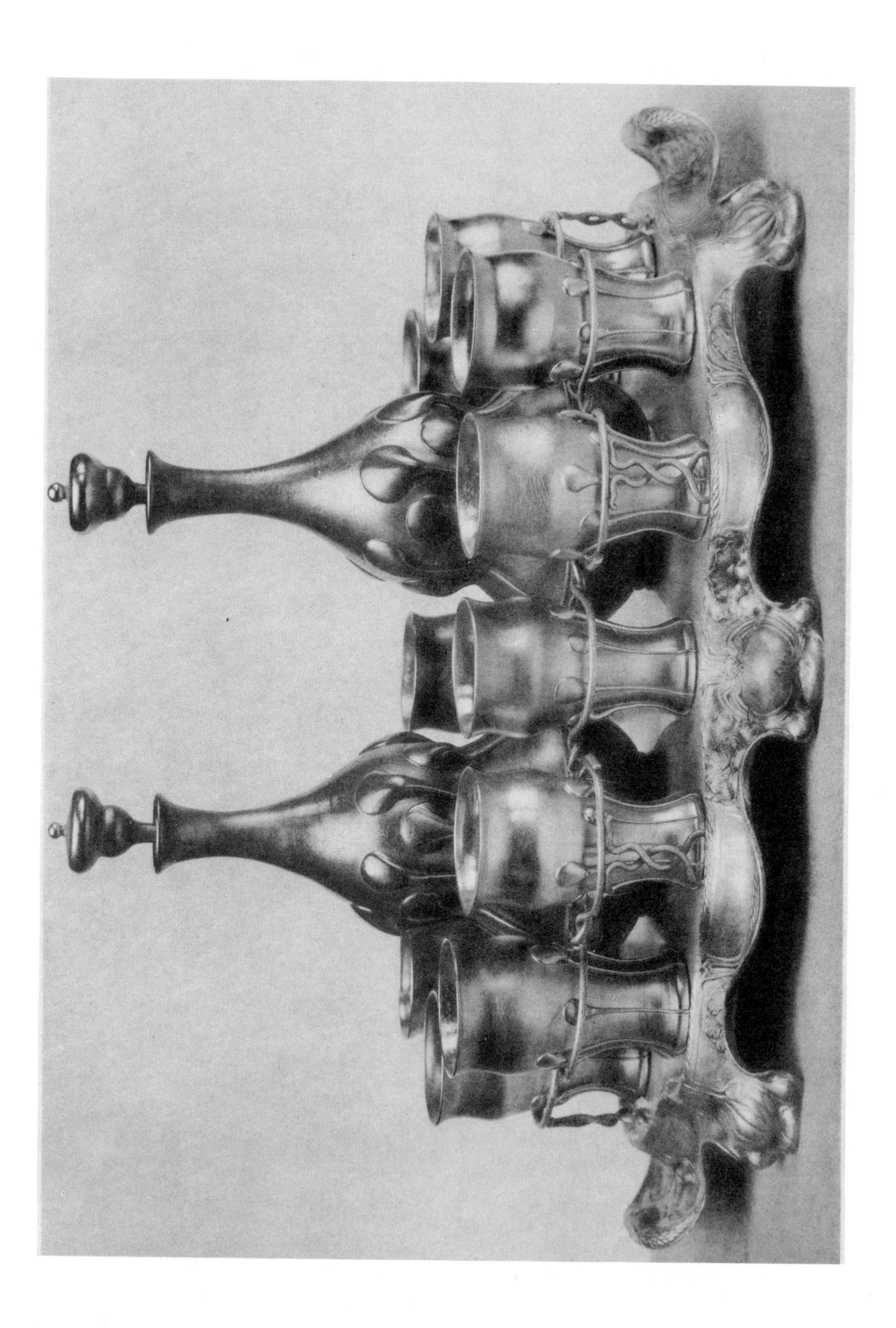

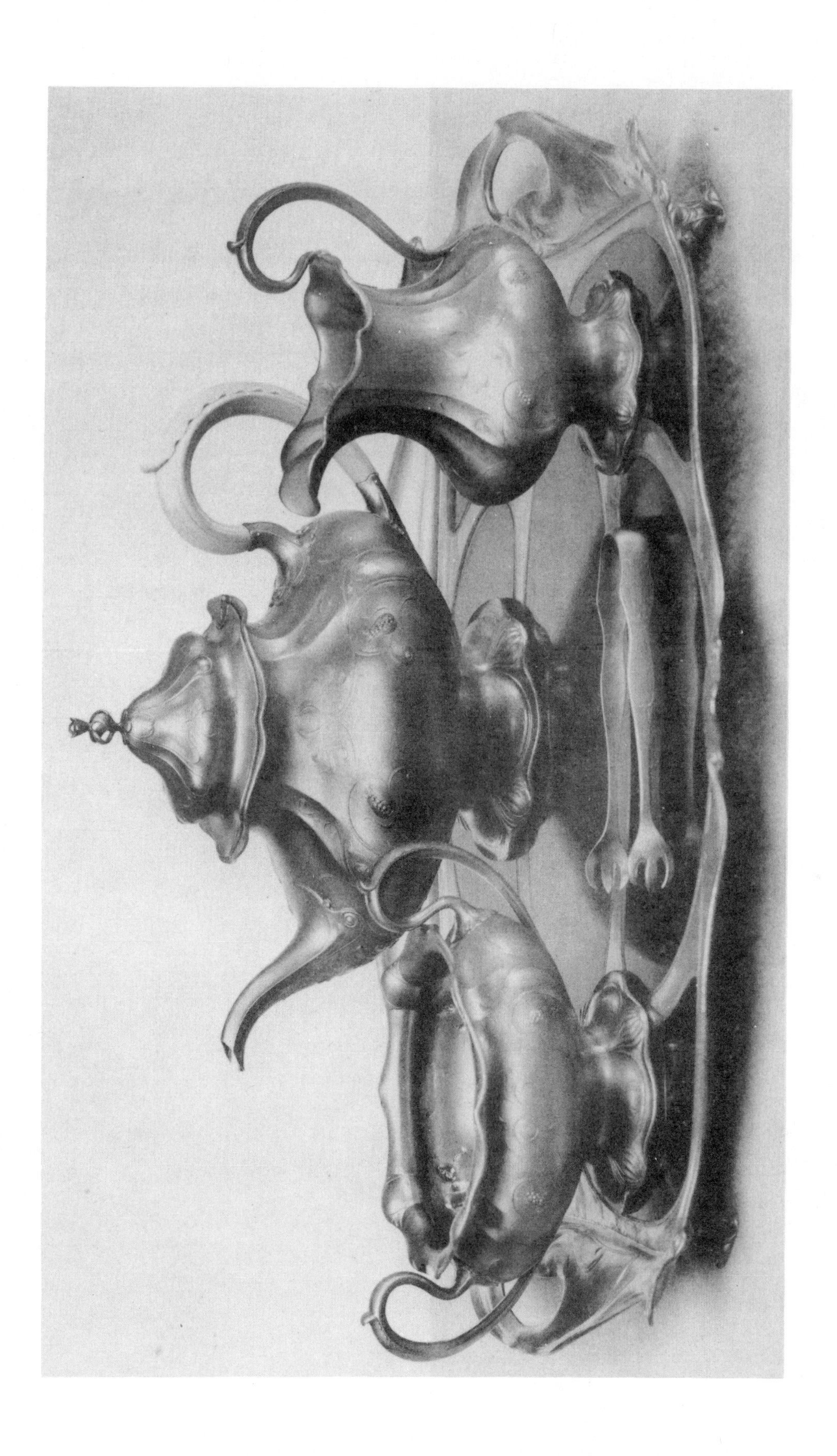

UNGER BROTHERS, 1904

The firm of Unger Brothers was first listed in Newark, New Jersey, city directories in 1881 although the two brothers, Eugene and Herman Unger, were listed separately as engravers as early as 1870. From April 17, 1872, to October 3, 1873, Herman Unger was listed with William C. J. Keen and Oscar Keen as partners in the firm of Unger & Keen, manufacturing jewelers. H. Unger & Co., manufacturing jewelers, was the listing from 1878 to 1879, with the partners being Eugene Unger, Frederick Unger and Herman Unger. Eugene Unger, manufacturing jeweler, was listed with H. Unger & Co., 1878–1879; with Unger Bros., 1881–1904; and as Unger & Christl, with J. Victor Christl and George W. Hagney, 1906–1909. Frederick Unger, also a manufacturing jeweler, was listed as working only from 1878 to 1879 with H. Unger & Co. Herman Unger, the only one of the brothers to be listed as a silversmith, was listed with Unger & Keen, 1872–1873; with H. Unger & Co., 1878–1879; and with Unger Bros., 1881–1910.

When the Unger Brothers company was formed in 1881, Herman Unger was president. Eugene Unger was listed as a member of the firm. They employed Philemon O. Dickinson, a painter of watch dials and an engraver; Otto Leigh; and Edward P. Beach, a painter who also served as vice-president and treasurer.

Rococo styles dominated their silverware designs for the first few years but by 1900 their catalogs included some of the favorite Art Nouveau motifs. Dresserware was perhaps their most important line, with a few of these designs being made in as many as 77 different pieces. They created designs of flowers with sinuous stems, blossoms and leaves, and women in swirling draperies and long flowing hair. The designs were given such names as "Stolen Kiss," "Lily," "Wild Rose," "Peep O' Day," "Love's Voyage," "Love's Dream," "He Loves Me," "Reine des Fleurs," "Le Secret des Fleurs," "Evangeline," "Dawn," "Man in the Moon," and "Bride of the Wave." Desk sets, ash trays, pocket flasks, cigarette cases, match boxes, flower vases and sewing articles were sometimes made in these same designs.

Compotes, berry bowls, trays, bonbon dishes and bread trays were made in flower designs of poppies, wild roses, daffodils, hibiscus, sweet peas, water lilies, iris, carnations and orchids. A few of these designs were also used for tea and coffee services.

The glass used for puff and vaseline jars was not made by the Ungers but it was cut in their factory.

The 1904 Unger Brothers catalog, reproduced in part here, contained 183 pages. It was necessary to reduce these pages by about one-half so that measurements of articles listed as full size are no longer accurate. The pages selected were chosen in order to give the full range of patterns and articles made. While it may be stretching a point to include hem gauges, cigar cutters, bag tags and book marks with holloware, these were chosen in preference to repetitious pages of bread trays, compotes and berry dishes.

In addition to the items reproduced, there were also the following: 14 hair brushes, 23 mirrors, 40 clothes brushes, 25 bonnet or ladies' brushes, 111 combs, 22 nail files, 23 button hooks, 13 shoe horns, 14 toothbrushes, 12 powder puffs, 7 cuticle knives, 8 corn knives, 1 hair curler, 20 steel sharpeners, 20 berry bowls, 2 tête-à-tête sets, 6 bread trays, 16 bonbon dishes, 9 candlesticks, 14 cups, 18 flasks, 1 desk set, 1 paperweight, 11 pen wipers, 14 rattles, 8 flower holders, 19 corks and cork screws, 3 chatelaine bags, 13 girdles, 40 garters, 48 side elastics and suspenders, 31 book marks, 48 puff and vaseline jars, 40 bonbon and chatelaine boxes, 46 scissors, 8 loving cups and 32 pages of jewelry.

The 1904 Unger Brothers catalog was an unusually unwieldy publication, measuring approximately 15 by 20 inches and bound in a flimsy paper cover. The photographic reproductions were not of good quality, and the full detail of many pieces is not revealed. Its size and the quality of the paper on which the original was printed are undoubtedly responsible for the numerous tears and smudges present in the copy from which the following reproductions were made.

UNGER · BRO'S
MANUFACTURING · JEWELERS
SILVERSMITHS
& GLASS CUTTERS
412-18 HALSEY ST
NEWARK. N.J.

STERLING SILVER

HAIR BRUSHES

ILLUSTRATIONS ACTUAL SIZE

"LE SECRETE DES FLEURS"
(Secret of the Flowers)
TOILET SET
Made in the following pieces
Design Patented

0561 Handle Mirror
0562 Ring Mirror
0563 Hair Brush
0582 Fancy Military Brush
0564 Military Brush
0565 Small Cloth Brush
0566 Small Velvet Brush
0567 Large Cloth Brush
0568 Large Hat Brush
0569 Large Bonnet Brush
0570 Small Hat Brush
0571 Small Nail Brush
0572 Small Pumice
0573 Handle Nail Brush
0574 Handle Nail Polisher
0575 Handle Pumice
0576 Small Bonnet Brush
0577 Ladies' Comb
0578 Gents' Comb
0579 Whisk
0583 Large Nail Polisher
0667 Small Vaseline Jar
0668 Medium Vaseline Jar
0669 Medium Puff Jar, prism cut
0670 Medium Fancy Puff Jar
0671 Large Puff Jar
0672 Talcum
0790 Large Talcum Bottle
0673 Tooth Brush Bottle
0674 Hair Pin Bottle
0675 Tooth Powder Bottle
0735 Jewel Case
0829 Soap Box
01115 Hook
01116 File
01119 Glove Stretcher
01120 Double Curler
01121 Single Curler
01122 Shoe Horn
01123 Tooth Brush
01124 Corn Knife
01126 Cuticle
01128 Pumice
01129 Nail Brush
01130 Tweezer
01924—6349 Cologne Bottle
02383 Straight Manicure Scissors
02384 Curved Manicure Scissors
02385 Straight Nail Scissors
02386 Curved Nail Scissors

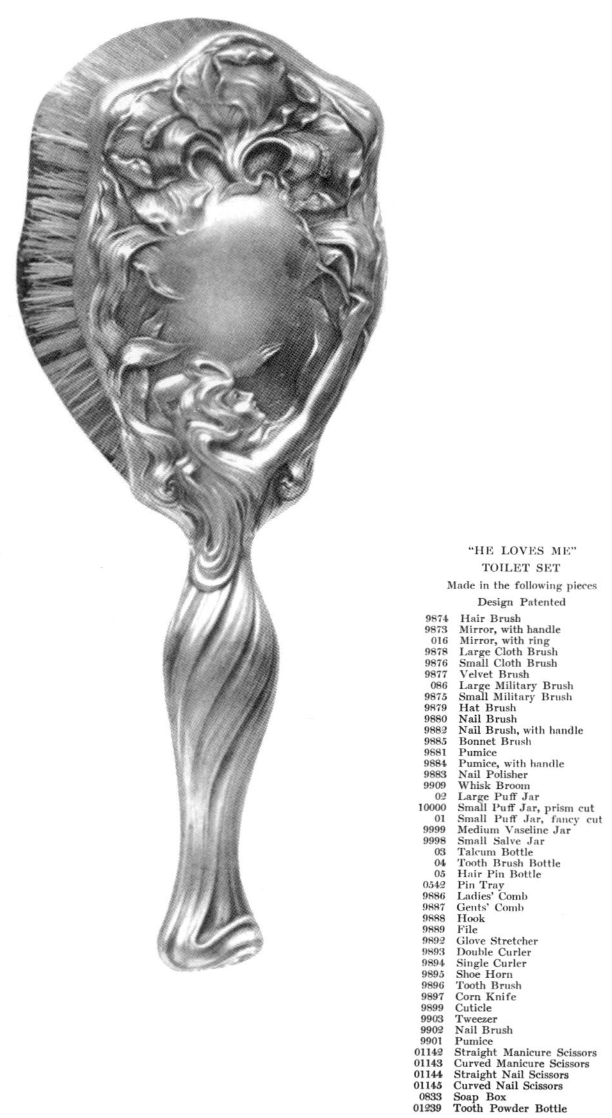

"HE LOVES ME"
TOILET SET
Made in the following pieces
Design Patented

9874 Hair Brush
9873 Mirror, with handle
016 Mirror, with ring
9878 Large Cloth Brush
9876 Small Cloth Brush
9877 Velvet Brush
086 Large Military Brush
9875 Small Military Brush
9879 Hat Brush
9880 Nail Brush
9882 Nail Brush, with handle
9885 Bonnet Brush
9881 Pumice
9884 Pumice, with handle
9883 Nail Polisher
9909 Whisk Broom
02 Large Puff Jar
10000 Small Puff Jar, prism cut
01 Small Puff Jar, fancy cut
9999 Medium Vaseline Jar
9998 Small Salve Jar
03 Talcum Bottle
04 Tooth Brush Bottle
05 Hair Pin Bottle
0542 Pin Tray
9886 Ladies' Comb
9887 Gents' Comb
9888 Hook
9889 File
9892 Glove Stretcher
9893 Double Curler
9894 Single Curler
9895 Shoe Horn
9896 Tooth Brush
9897 Corn Knife
9899 Cuticle
9903 Tweezer
9902 Nail Brush
9901 Pumice
01142 Straight Manicure Scissors
01143 Curved Manicure Scissors
01144 Straight Nail Scissors
01145 Curved Nail Scissors
0833 Soap Box
01239 Tooth Powder Bottle

9874
French Gray Finish

"REINE DES FLEURS"
(Queen of the Flowers)
TOILET SET
Made in the following pieces
Design Patented

0618 Handle Mirror
0619 Ring Mirror
0620 Hair Brush
0621 Military Brush
0622 Small Cloth Brush
0623 Velvet Brush
0624 Large Cloth Brush
0625 Large Hat Brush
0626 Large Bonnet Brush
0627 Small Hat Brush
0628 Small Nail Brush
0629 Small Pumice
0630 Handle Nail Brush
0631 Handle Nail Polisher
0632 Handle Pumice
0633 Bonnet Brush
0634 Ladies' Comb
0635 Gents' Comb
0636 Whisk
0637 Large Fancy Military Brush
0638 Large Nail Polisher
0676 Small Vaseline Jar
0677 Medium Vaseline Jar
0678 Medium Puff Jar, prism cut
0679 Medium Puff Jar, fancy cut
0680 Large Puff Jar
0681 Talcum Bottle
0791 Talcum Bottle, large
0682 Tooth Brush Bottle
0683 Hair Pin Bottle
0684 Tooth Powder Bottle
0736 Jewel Case
0830 Soap Box
01193 Hook
01194 File
01197 Glove Stretcher
01198 Double Curler
01199 Single Curler
01200 Shoe Horn
01201 Tooth Brush
01202 Corn Knife
01204 Cuticle
01206 Pumice
01207 Nail Brush
01208 Tweezer
01923—6349 Cologne Bottle
02383 Straight Manicure Scissors
02384 Curved Manicure Scissors
02385 Straight Nail Scissors
02386 Curved Nail Scissors

0620
French Gray Finish

STERLING SILVER

HAIR BRUSHES

ILLUSTRATIONS ACTUAL SIZE

9836
French Gray Finish

"DAWN"

TOILET SET

Made in the following pieces

Design Patented

9836 Hair Brush
9835 Mirror, with handle
015 Mirror, Ring
9838 Large Cloth Brush
9839 Small Cloth Brush
9840 Velvet Brush
9837 Military Brush
9841 Hat Brush
9842 Nail Brush
9845 Nail Brush, with handle
9867 Bonnet Brush
9843 Pumice
9846 Pumice, with handle
9844 Nail Polisher
030 Whisk Broom
94 Medium Puff Jar
92 Small Puff Jar, prism cut
93 Small Puff Jar, fancy cut
9991 Medium Vaseline Jar
9990 Small Salve Jar
9995 Talcum Powder Bottle
9996 Tooth Brush Bottle
9997 Hair Pin Bottle
034 Pin Tray
036 Jewel Case
9847 Ladies' Comb
9865 Gents' Comb
9848 Hook
9849 File
9852 Glove Stretcher
9853 Double Curler
9854 Single Curler
9855 Shoe Horn
9856 Tooth Brush
9857 Corn Knife
9859 Cuticle
9863 Tweezer
9861 Pumice
9862 Nail Brush
01142 Straight Manicure Scissors
01143 Curved Manicure Scissors
01144 Straight Nail Scissors
01145 Curved Nail Scissors
0832 Soap Box
01238 Tooth Powder Bottle

"LOVE'S DREAM"

TOILET SET

Made in the following pieces

Design Patented

7522 Large Hair Brush
7523 Medium Hair Brush
7524 Small Hair Brush
7525 Large Mirror, with handle
7527 Medium Mirror, with handle
7529 Small Mirror, with handle
7526 Large Mirror, ring handle
7528 Medium Mirror, ring handle
7530 Small Mirror, ring handle
7533 Large Cloth Brush
7531 Small Cloth Brush
7532 Velvet Brush
0528 Large Military Brush
7597 Medium Military Brush
7534 Large Hat Brush
7540 Small Hat Brush
7535 Large Nail Brush
7541 Small Nail Brush
7537 Large Nail Brush, with handle
7543 Small Nail Brush, with handle
7714 Large Bonnet Brush
7574 Medium Bonnet Brush
7536 Large Pumice
7542 Small Pumice
7538 Large Pumice, with handle
7544 Small Pumice, with handle
7539 Large Nail Polisher
7545 Small Nail Polisher
6366 Medium Puff Jar
6141 Small Puff Jar, prism cut
6152 Small Puff Jar, fancy cut
6129 Large Vaseline Jar
6118 Medium Vaseline Jar
6368 Small Salve Jar
0431 Tooth Powder Bottle
6359 Large Talcum Bottle
8783 Small Talcum Bottle
6365 Tooth Brush Bottle
6361 Hair Pin Bottle
7685/6349 Cologne Bottle
6398 Hair Receiver
7555 Corn Knife
7557 Cuticle
7586 Tweezer
7559 Pumice
7560 Nail Brush
6944 Straight Manicure Scissors
6945 Curved Manicure Scissors
6946 Straight Nail Scissors
6952 Curved Nail Scissors
7926 Tooth Brush Case
7923 Pin Cushion
7925 Curling Iron Lamp
7615 Whisk Broom
6367 Large Puff Jar
6278 Salt Jar
7928 Pin Tray
8071 Puff
7635 Soap Box
8803 Jewel Case
8807 Jewel Case
8806 Jewel Case
7561 Ladies' Comb
7623 Gents' Comb
7546 Hook
7547 File
7550 Glove Stretcher
7551 Curler, double
7552 Curler, single
7553 Shoe Horn
7554 Tooth Brush
0834 Soap Box

7522
French Gray Finish

"EVANGELINE"

TOILET SET

Made in the following pieces

Design Patented

9726 Hair Brush
9724 Mirror, with handle
014 Mirror, with ring
9728 Large Cloth Brush
9729 Small Cloth Brush
9730 Velvet Brush
9727 Military Brush
9731 Hat Brush
9732 Nail Brush
9735 Nail Brush, with handle
9737 Bonnet Brush
9733 Pumice
9736 Pumice, with handle
9734 Nail Polisher
9869 Whisk Broom
9986 Medium Puff Jar
9984 Small Puff Jar, prism cut
9985 Small Puff Jar, fancy cut
9983 Medium Vaseline Jar
9982 Small Salve Jar
9987 Talcum Powder Bottle
9988 Tooth Brush Bottle
9989 Hair Pin Bottle
0155 Pin Tray
037 Jewel Case
9725 Ladies' Comb
9866 Gents' Comb
9738 Hook
9739 File
9744 Glove Stretcher
9745 Double Curler
9746 Single Curler
9747 Shoe Horn
9748 Tooth Brush
9742 Corn Knife
9749 Cuticle
9753 Tweezer
9751 Pumice
9752 Nail Brush
01142 Straight Manicure Scissors
01143 Curved Manicure Scissors
01144 Straight Nail Scissors
01145 Curved Nail Scissors
0835 Soap Box
0540 Brush and Comb Tray
01237 Tooth Powder Bottle

9726
French Gray Finish

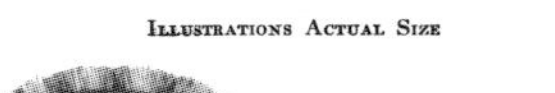

STERLING SILVER

HAIR BRUSHES

ILLUSTRATIONS ACTUAL SIZE

"ART NOUVEAU" TOILET SET

Made in the following pieces

8149 Hair Brush
8147 Mirror, with handle
8148 Mirror, with ring
8150 Large Cloth Brush
8151 Small Cloth Brush
8152 Velvet Brush
8153 Military Brush
8156 Hat Brush
8157 Nail Brush
8160 Nail Brush, with handle
8178 Bonnet Brush
8158 Pumice
8161 Pumice, with handle
8159 Nail Polisher
8196 Whisk Broom
6458 Medium Puff Jar
6456 Small Puff Jar, prism cut
6457 Small Puff Jar, fancy cut
6455 Medium Vaseline Jar
8344 Small Salve Jar
8154 Ladies' Comb
8155 Gents' Comb
8162 Hook
8163 File
8166 Glove Stretcher
8167 Curler, double
8168 Curler, single
8169 Shoe Horn
8170 Tooth Brush
8171 Corn Knife
8173 Cuticle
8177 Tweezer
8175 Pumice
8176 **Nail Brush**

French Gray Finish
8149

"CUPID" TOILET SET

Made in the following pieces

Design Patented

2879 Large Hair Brush
2880 Medium Hair Brush
2881 Small Hair Brush
3091 Medium Mirror, with handle
5347 Small Mirror, with handle
3092 Medium Mirror, with ring
5346 Small Mirror, with ring
3079 Large Cloth Brush
2945 Small Cloth Brush
3081 Velvet Brush
3082 Large Military Brush
3227 Small Military Brush
3087 Hat Rim Brush
2932 Large Hat Brush
2947 Small Hat Brush
3083 Large Nail Brush
2946 Small Nail Brush
3084 Large Nail Brush, with handle
3080 Small Nail Brush, with handle
2992 Large Bonnet Brush
2991 Medium Bonnet Brush
2990 Small Bonnet Brush
3086 Large Pumice, with handle
3085 Small Pumice, with handle
2985 Large Pumice
2948 Small Pumice
2994 Large Nail Polisher
3051 Small Nail Polisher
3096 Whisk Broom
3470 Small Puff Jar, fancy cut
2212 Large Salve Jar, plain
3302 Large Salve Jar, prism
3323 Medium Salve Jar, prism
2200 Small Salve Jar, plain
3843 Large Tooth Powder Bottle
2514 Small Tooth Powder Bottle
3884 Tooth Brush Bottle
3188 Large Glove Stretcher
3186 Medium Glove Stretcher
3187 Small Glove Stretcher
1165 Large Curler, double
2795 Medium Curler, double
1166 Large Curler, single
2794 Medium Curler, single
1232 Large Shoe Horn
2793 Medium Shoe Horn
2583 Small Shoe Horn
1163 Large Tooth Brush
1164 Large Corn Knife
2792 Medium Corn Knife
1923 Small Corn Knife
3481 Large Pumice
5371 Medium Pumice
2921 Large Nail Brush
461 Straight Manicure Scissors
462 Curved Manicure Scissors
463 Straight Nail Scissors
464 Curved Nail Scissors
3784 Talcum Bottle
3102 Pin Tray
5341 Puff
5319 Soap Box
3228½ Ladies' Comb
3229½ Gents' Comb
3230 Barber Comb
1159 Large Hook
2788 Medium Hook
1168 Small Hook
1158 Large File
2787 Medium File
1167 Small File
1284 Large Cuticle
2791 Medium Cuticle
1169 Small Cuticle
1933 Large Tweezer
2789 Medium Tweezer
1899 Small Tweezer

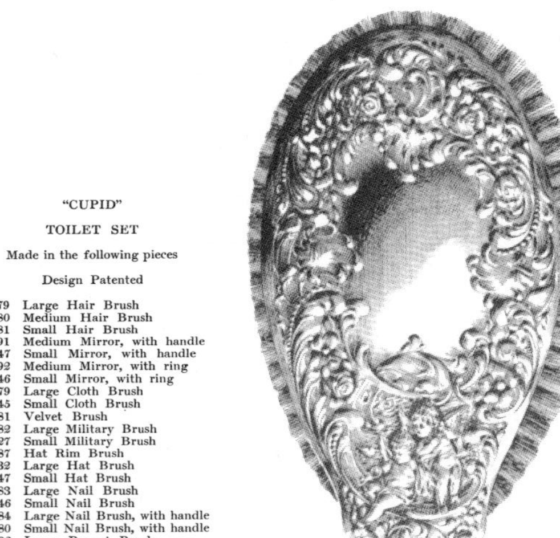

Bright Polished
2879

"TULIP" TOILET SET

Made in the following pieces

7294 Hair Brush
7296 Mirror, with handle
7295 Mirror, with ring
7297 Large Cloth Brush
7298 Small Cloth Brush
7299 Velvet Brush
7300 Military Brush
7614 Hat Rim Brush
7306 Large Hat Brush
7236 Small Hat Brush
7307 Large Nail Brush
7235 Small Nail Brush
7303 Large Nail Brush, with handle
7264 Small Nail Brush, with handle
7301 Bonnet Brush
7305 Large Pumice
7237 Small Pumice
7304 Large Pumice, with handle
7266 Small Pumice, with handle
7302 Large Nail Polisher
7265 Small Nail Polisher
7489 Whisk Broom
6332 Puff Jar, prism cut
6333 Puff Jar, fancy cut
7308 Ladies' Comb
7309 Gents' Comb
7311 Large Hook
7445 Small Hook
7310 Large File
7446 Small File
7314 Large Glove Stretcher
7454 Small Glove Stretcher
7315 Large Curler, double
7453 Small Curler, double
7316 Large Curler, single
7452 Small Curler, single
7317 Large Shoe Horn
7447 Small Shoe Horn
7318 Large Tooth Brush
7451 Small Tooth Brush
7319 Large Corn Knife
7450 Small Corn Knife
7321 Large Cuticle
7448 Small Cuticle
7585 Large Tweezer
7323 Large Pumice
7324 Large Nail Brush
8114 **Tooth Brush Case**

French Gray Finish
7294

"WATER-LILY" TOILET SET

Made in the following pieces

8216 Hair Brush
8215 Mirror, with handle
047 Mirror, with ring
8218 Large Cloth Brush
8219 Small Cloth Brush
8220 Velvet Brush
8217 Military Brush
8221 Hat Brush
8222 Nail Brush
8225 Nail Brush, with handle
8227 Bonnet Brush
8223 Pumice
8226 Pumice, with handle
8224 Nail Polisher
9640 Puff Jar, prism cut
9641 Puff Jar, fancy cut
9981 Medium Vaseline Jar
9980 Small Salve Jar
8228 Ladies' Comb
8229 Gents' Comb
8231 Hook
8232 File
8237 Glove Stretcher
8238 Curler, double
8239 Curler, single
8240 Shoe Horn
8241 Tooth Brush
8235 Corn Knife
8242 Cuticle
8246 **Tweezer**

French Gray Finish
8216

STERLING SILVER

MIRRORS

ILLUSTRATIONS ACTUAL SIZE

0889

STOLEN KISS
Handle Mirror shows front of design
and Ring Mirror shows back of design
French Gray Finish
Copyrighted

0890 Stolen Kiss Back View

0952
Wild Rose
French Gray Finish

0910 Lily
0911 Ring
French Gray Finish

MIRRORS

Illustrations Actual Size

8147 Art Nouveau

8148 Art Nouveau

9905

All French Gray Finish

7295 Tulip

8117 Love's Voyage
8193 Ring

STERLING SILVER

MILITARY BRUSHES

ILLUSTRATIONS ACTUAL SIZE

0892 Stolen Kiss

0913 Lily

0939 Old English Polished

0637 Reine des Fleurs

0582 Les Secrete des Fleurs

All French Gray Finish except 0939

086 He Loves Me

8217 Waterlily

0738 Peep o' Day

8153 Art Nouveau

0528 Love's Dream

STERLING SILVER

MILITARY BRUSHES

Illustrations Actual Size

0893 Stolen Kiss

0914 Lily

7597 Love's Dream

0564 Les Secrete des Fleurs

0621 Reine des Fleurs

9875 He Loves Me

All French Gray Finish

9727 Evangeline

9837 Dawn

0588 Peep o' Day

0985 Man in Moon

8188 Indian

8119 Love's Voyage

STERLING SILVER

CLOTH, VELVET AND HAT BRUSHES

Illustrations Actual Size

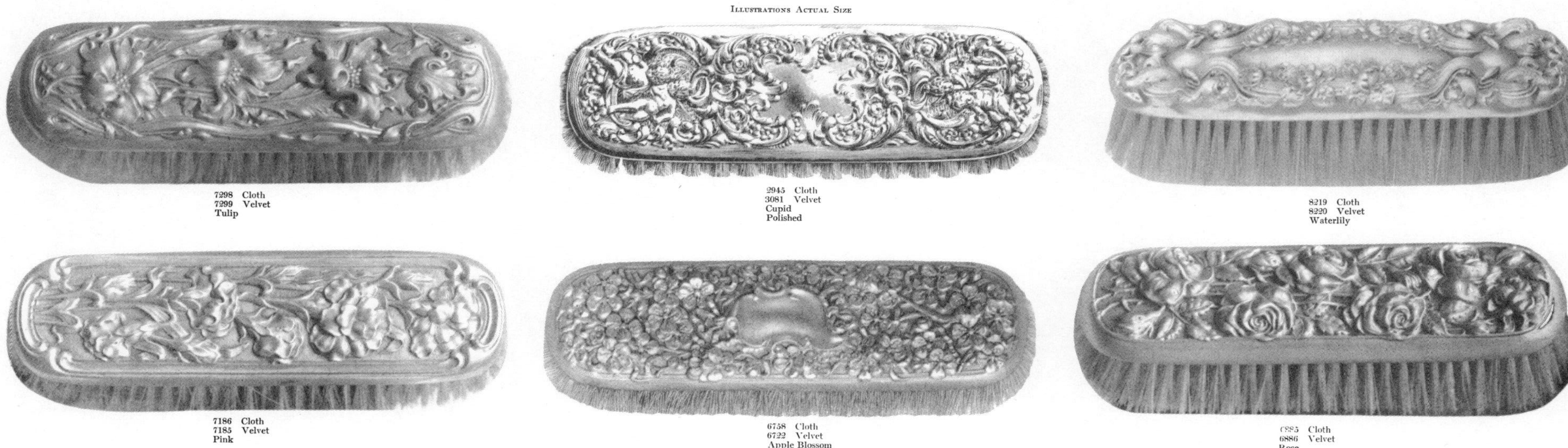

7298 Cloth
7299 Velvet
Tulip

2945 Cloth
3081 Velvet
Cupid
Polished

8219 Cloth
8220 Velvet
Waterlily

7186 Cloth
7185 Velvet
Pink

6758 Cloth
6722 Velvet
Apple Blossom

6885 Cloth
6886 Velvet
Rose

6747 Bride of the Wave

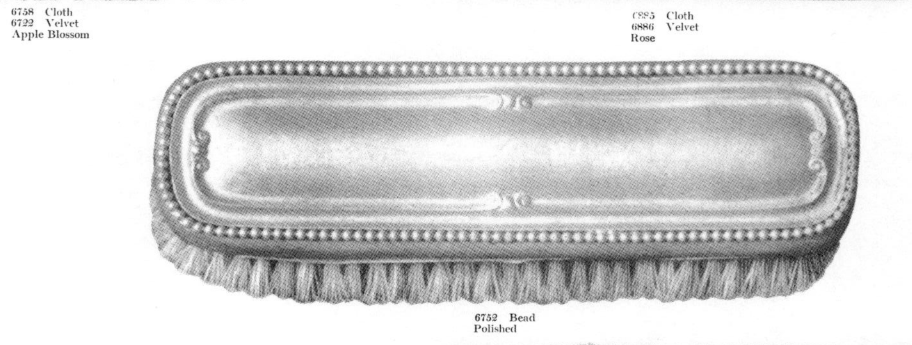

6752 Bead
Polished

7614 Tulip

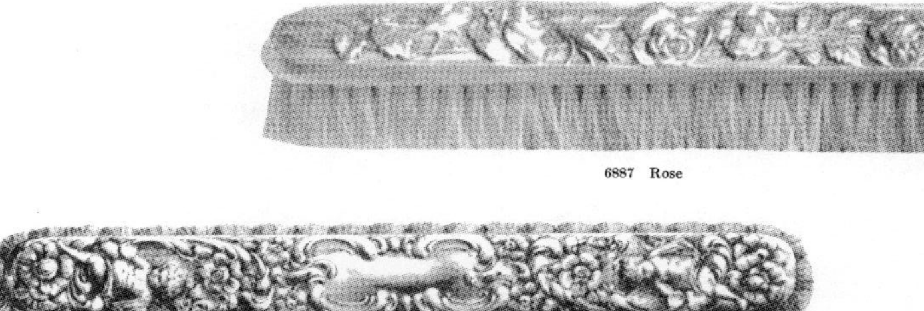

6887 Rose

French Gray Finish

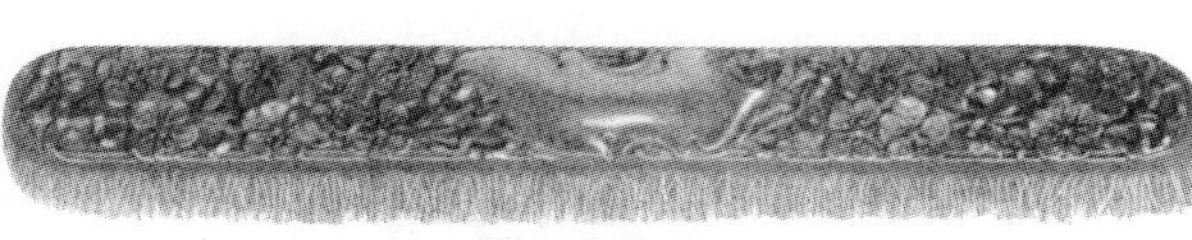

6755 Apple Blossom

3087 Cupid Polished

STERLING SILVER

WHISK BROOMS

7615 Love's Dream

8196 Art Nouveau

4293

0601 Peep o' Day

8194 Love's Voyage

7489 Tulip

4312

STERLING SILVER

NAIL POLISHERS

Illustrations Actual Size

0899 Stolen Kiss
0904 Size smaller

0920 Lily
0925 Size smaller

9734 Evangeline

0948 Old English

0583 Les Secrete des Fleurs
0574 Size smaller

0596 Peep o' Day

9844 Dawn

0638 Reine des Fleurs
0631 Size smaller

7302 Tulip

9883 He Loves Me

2994 Cupid

8224 Waterlily

3426 Floral

8159 Art Nouveau

7539 Love's Dream

8127 Love's Voyage

3319 Floral

7545 Love's Dream

7265 Tulip

2486 Rococo

3051 Cupid

2487 Rococo

STERLING SILVER

TOILET ARTICLES

ILLUSTRATIONS ACTUAL SIZE

Top of Talcum Bottle

8113 Tooth Brush Case

8114 Tooth Brush Case

7950 Tooth Brush Case

SOAP BOX
0834 Soap Box

0829	Les Secrete des Fleurs	0833	He Loves Me
0830	Reine des Fleurs	0835	Evangeline
0831	Peep-o'-Day	0836	Indian
0832	Dawn	02508	Stolen Kiss

7926 Tooth Brush Case

0646 Tooth Brush Case

3409 Tooth Brush Case

0514 All Silver Tooth Powder Bottle

0299 All Silver Talcum Bottle

0611 Hair Pin Case

Side View

517 Hair Pin Case

1462 1206

1421½ Tooth Brush Holder

01214 Hair Pin Case

0723 Papier Poudre Holder (Face Powder Book)

5319 Soap Box

516 Hair Pin Case

02020 Tooth Brush Holder

1517 1367

POCKET AND GENT'S COMBS

Illustrations Actual Size

6875 Pink

6900 Rose

6792 Apple Blossom

7335

9914

5878

1206

2662 Rococo

3229 Cupid

3256 Floral

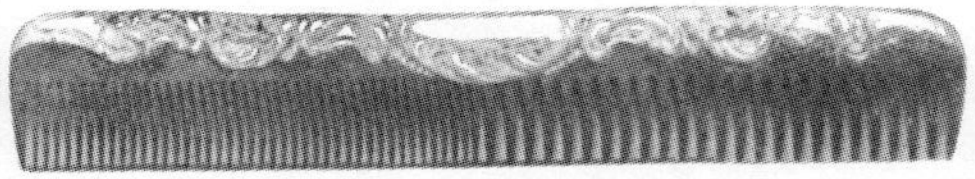

3230 Cupid

1367

5194

2660 Rococo

5497

3257 Floral

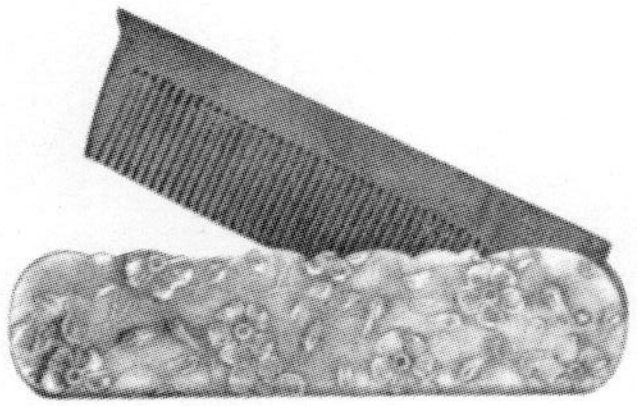

01213

5876

402

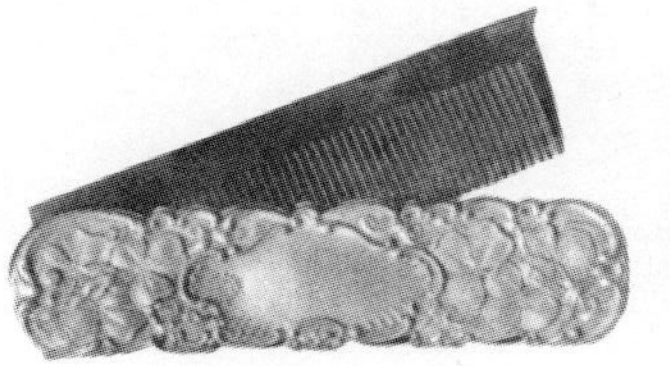

6924

021

STERLING SILVER

HE LOVES ME TOILET SET

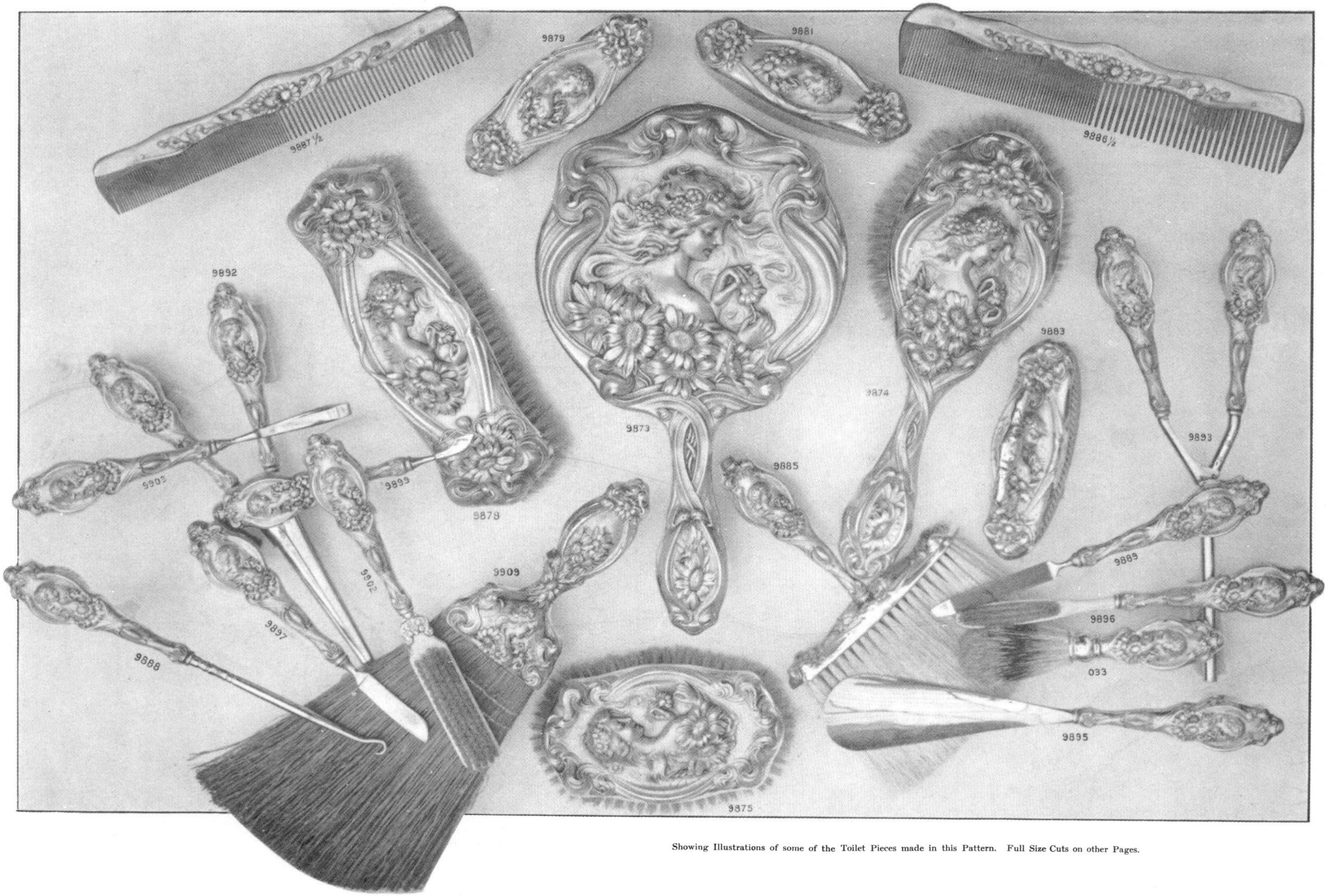

9887½ 9879 9881 9886½

9892 9873 9874 9883 9893

9903 9899 9878 9885

9909 9889 9896 033

9897 9902 9888 9895

9875

Showing Illustrations of some of the Toilet Pieces made in this Pattern. Full Size Cuts on other Pages.

STERLING SILVER

EVANGELINE TOILET SET

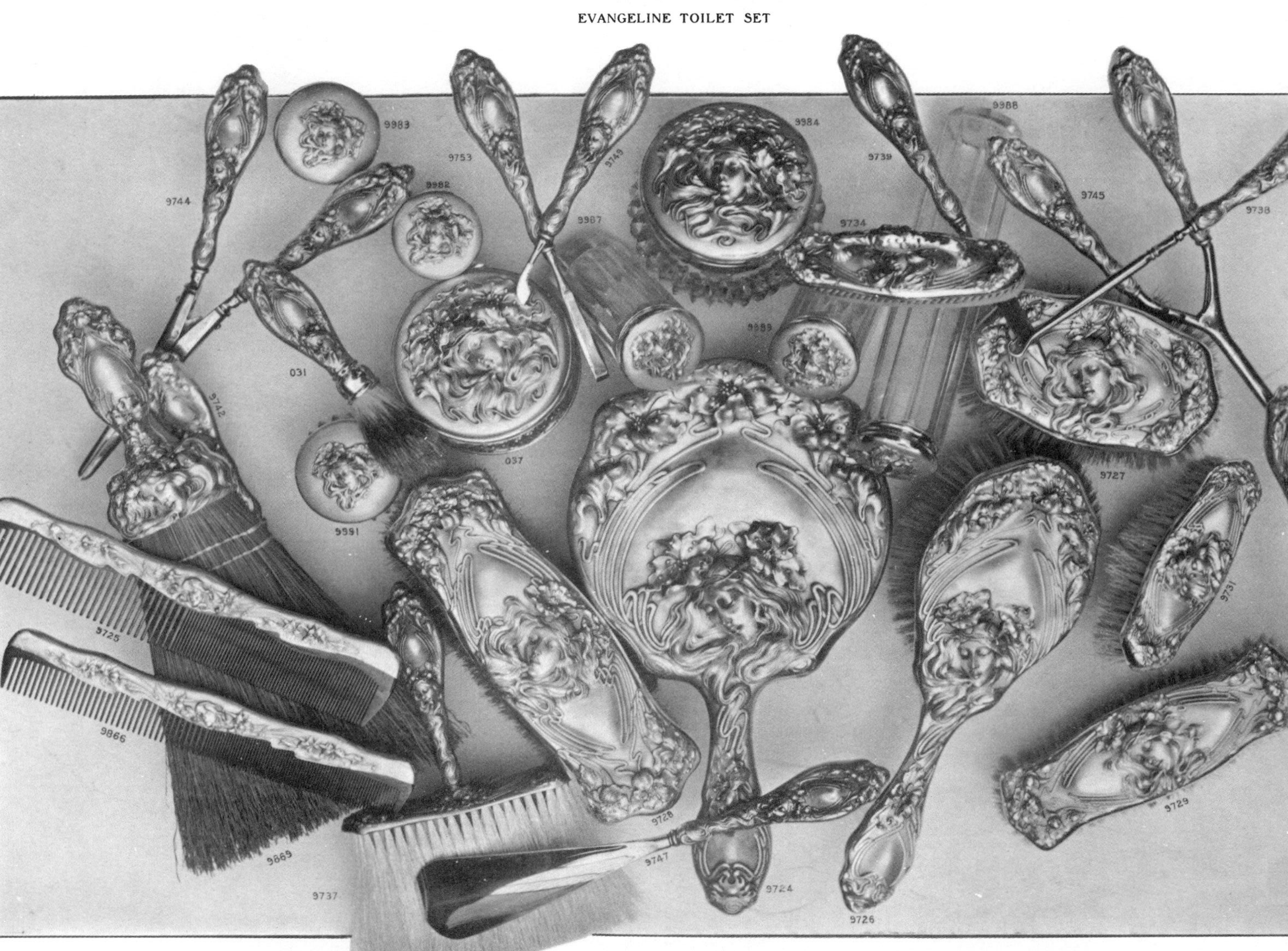

Showing Illustrations of some of the Toilet Pieces made in this Pattern. Full Size Cuts on other Pages.

STERLING SILVER

DAWN TOILET SET

Showing Illustrations of Toilet Pieces made in this Pattern. Full Size Cuts on other Pages.

STERLING SILVER

LOVE'S DREAM TOILET SET

Showing Illustrations of Toilet Pieces made in this Pattern. Full Size Cuts on other Pages.

STERLING SILVER

BABY BRUSHES AND COMBS

Illustrations Actual Size

8325

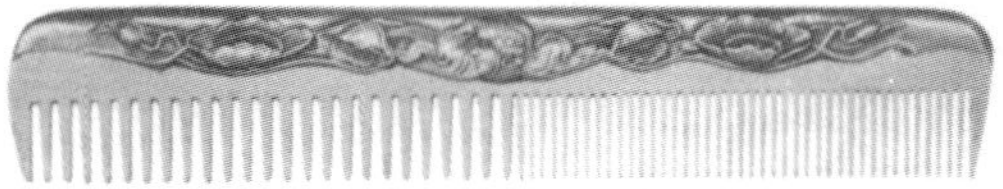

02397

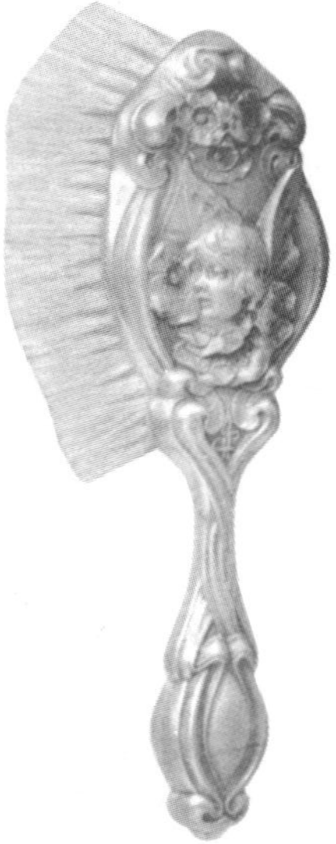

0794

0793

8182

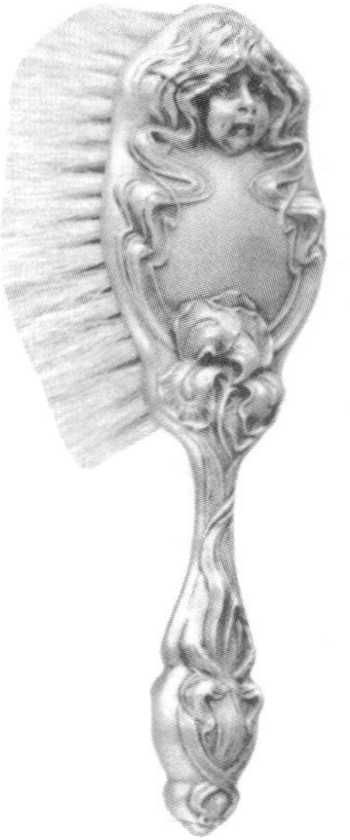

0795

1173

1174

3097

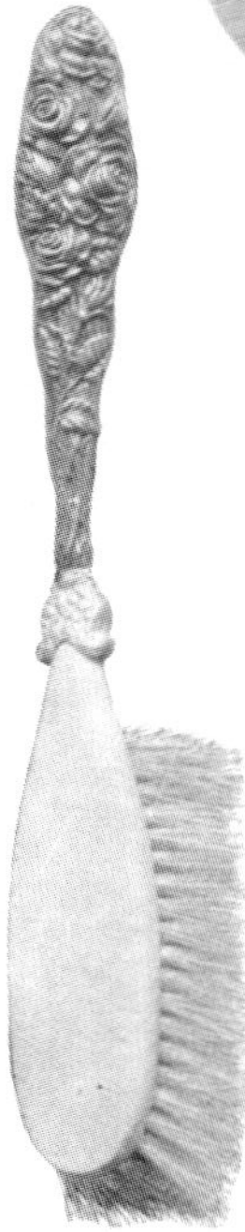

7427
7426 Comb to Match

7443
7442 Comb to match

7620

7621

STERLING  SILVER

PAPER CUTTERS

ILLUSTRATIONS ACTUAL SIZE

01922

0644 Paper Cutter

7951 7252 7924 7952 9810 7250 02398 01729 9809 9957 9811 5880 7251 7319

STERLING SILVER

PEARL PAPER CUTTERS

ILLUSTRATIONS ACTUAL SIZE

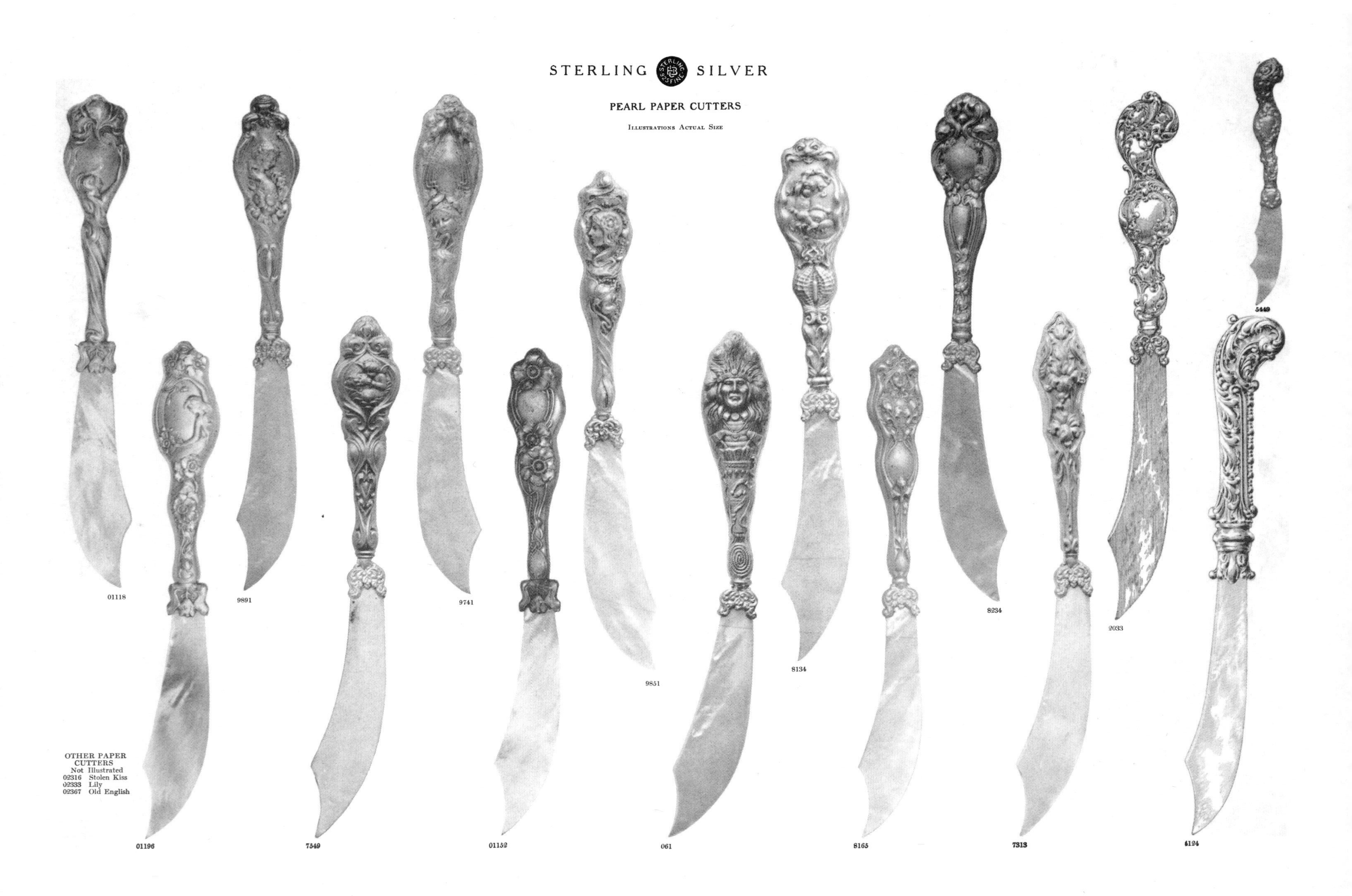

OTHER PAPER CUTTERS
Not Illustrated
02316 Stolen Kiss
02333 Lily
02367 Old English

PAPER CUTTERS AND ERASERS

Illustrations Actual Size

01830 01833 01829

JAN. 01817 FEB. 01818 MAR. 01819 APR. 01820 MAY 01821 JUNE 01822

01831 01798 01832 01919

BIRTHDAY PAPER CUTTERS

JULY 01823 AUG. 01824 SEPT. 01825 OCT. 01826 NOV. 01827 DEC. 01828

7558 7322

Other Erasers not Illustrated
02325 Stolen Kiss
02342 Lily
02354 Lily, small
02376 Old English

2790 7433 1162 3288 1170 2779 8174 8143

STERLING SILVER

ILLUSTRATIONS ACTUAL SIZE

SEALS

01125 01203 7556 9743 9858 9518 068 01159 8236 8141 8172

8892 02227 7341 01727 2801 1161

Other Seals not Illustrated
02323 Stolen Kiss
02340 Lily
02354 Lily, small
02376 Old English

Other Roller Blotters not Illustrated
02329 Stolen Kiss
02346 Lily
02380 Old English
01148 Les Secrete des Fleurs
01209 Reine des Fleurs
9904 He Loves Me
9864 Dawn
9754 Evangeline
01165 Peep o' Day
8195 Love's Voyage
2575 Cupid
7600 Tulip
8247 Waterlily

8197
Blotter

4023
Stamp Moistener

2802

9556
Wax Holder

1171

4026

Stamp Moisteners 01799

7600
Blotter

STERLING SILVER

TEA SETS

FIVE-PIECE TEA SETS

Showing Coffee Pots of each set actual size; other pieces illustrated half-size.

STERLING SILVER

COFFEE SETS

Illustrations Actual Size

9917 Cream

8090 Cream

THREE-PIECE COFFEE SET
Illustrations Actual Size

8088 Coffee

9916 Sugar

8089 Sugar

STERLING SILVER

FRENCH COFFEE SETS

Illustrations Actual Size

7589 Coffee

7688 Coffee Set Tray

7592 Coffee

7591 Cream

7590 Sugar

3378 Sugar

3379 Cream

BERRY BOWLS

Illustrations Actual Size

0848 Side View

0848

Solid Backs

0870

0870 Side View

BERRY BOWL

Illustrations Actual Size

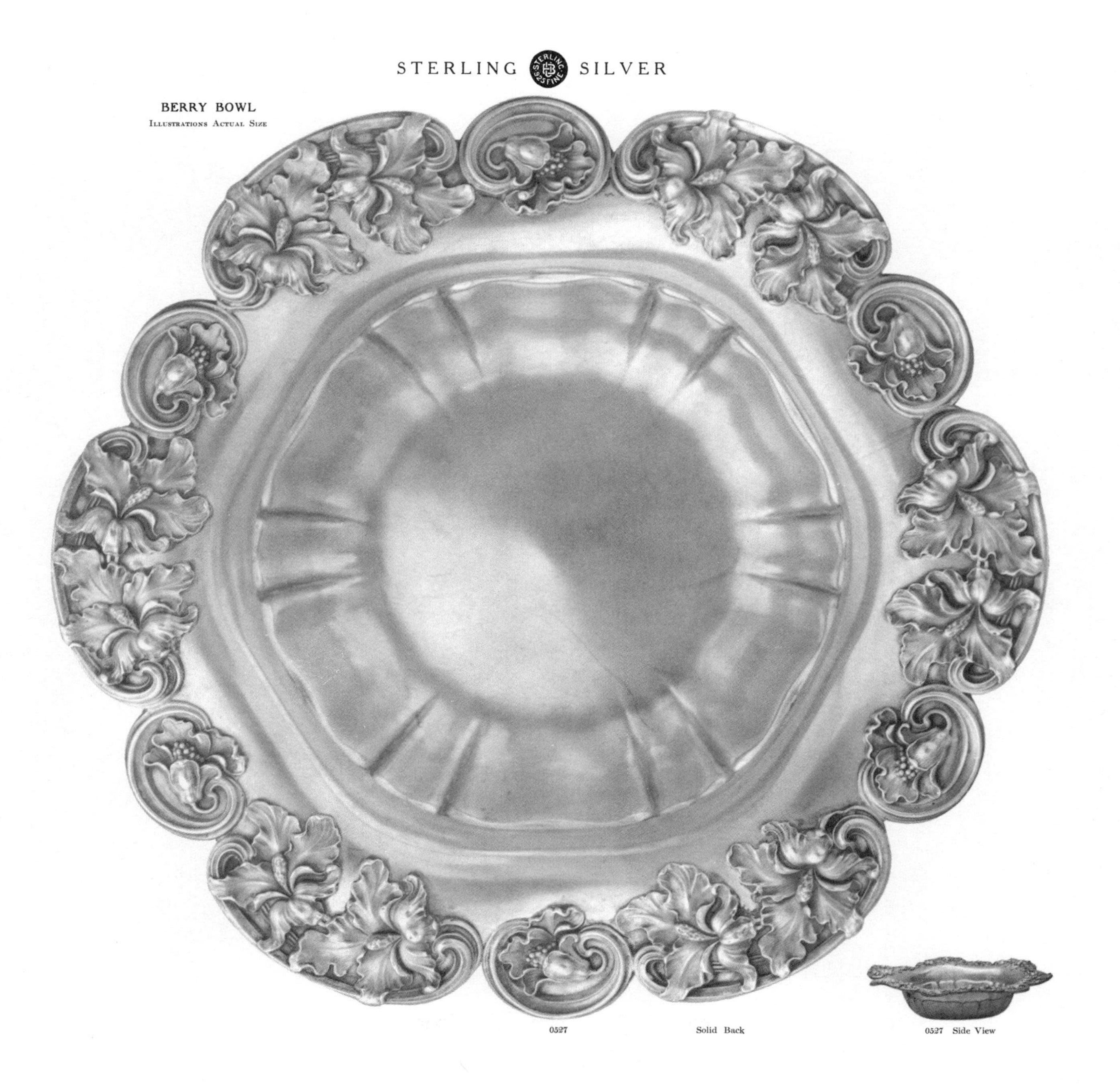

0527 Solid Back

0527 Side View

BERRY BOWLS

Illustrations Actual Size

0848 Side View

0848

Solid Backs

0870

0870 Side View

STERLING SILVER

BERRY BOWLS

Illustrations Actual Size

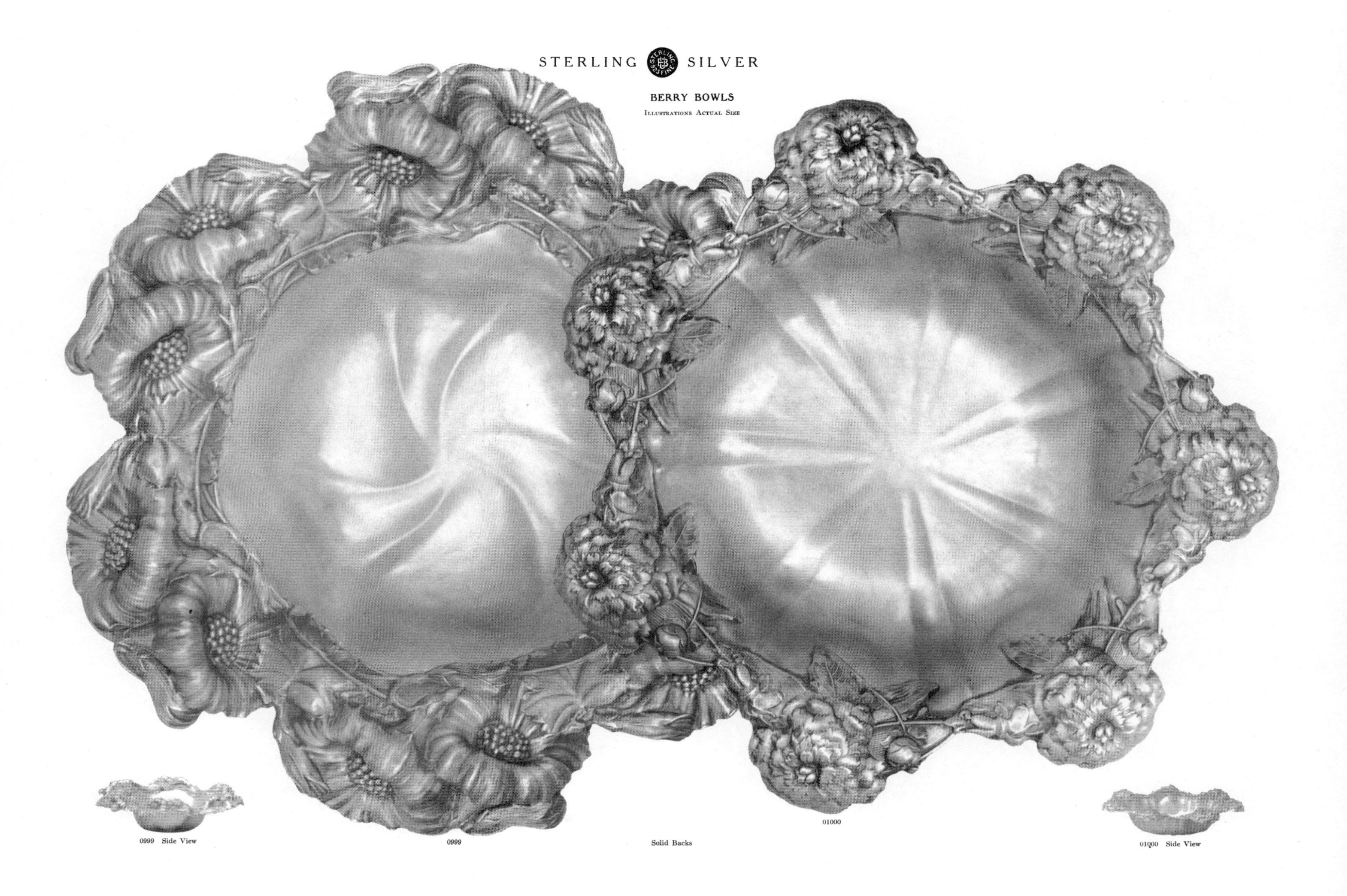

0999 Side View

0999

Solid Backs

01000

01000 Side View

BERRY BOWLS

Illustrations Actual Size

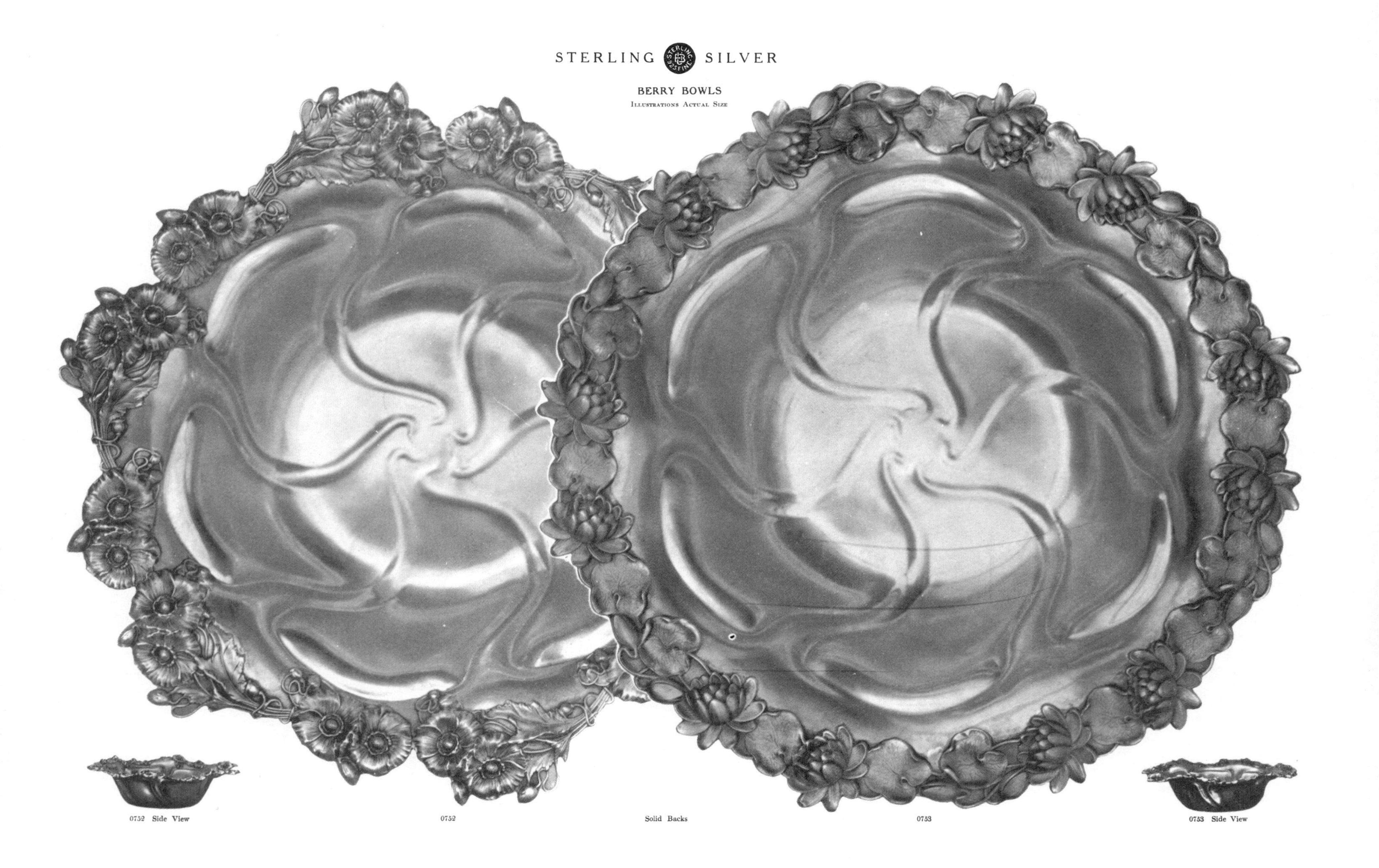

0752 Side View | 0752 | Solid Backs | 0753 | 0753 Side View

BERRY BOWLS

Illustrations Actual Size

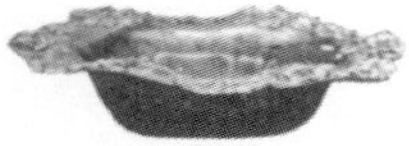

0520 Side View

0520

Solid Backs

0581

0581 Side View

Illustrations Actual Size

SERVING TRAY

BERRY DISH

8027

Hollow Backs

8099

STERLING SILVER

BREAD TRAY

Illustrations Actual Size

0502 Side View

BREAD TRAYS

Illustrations Actual Size

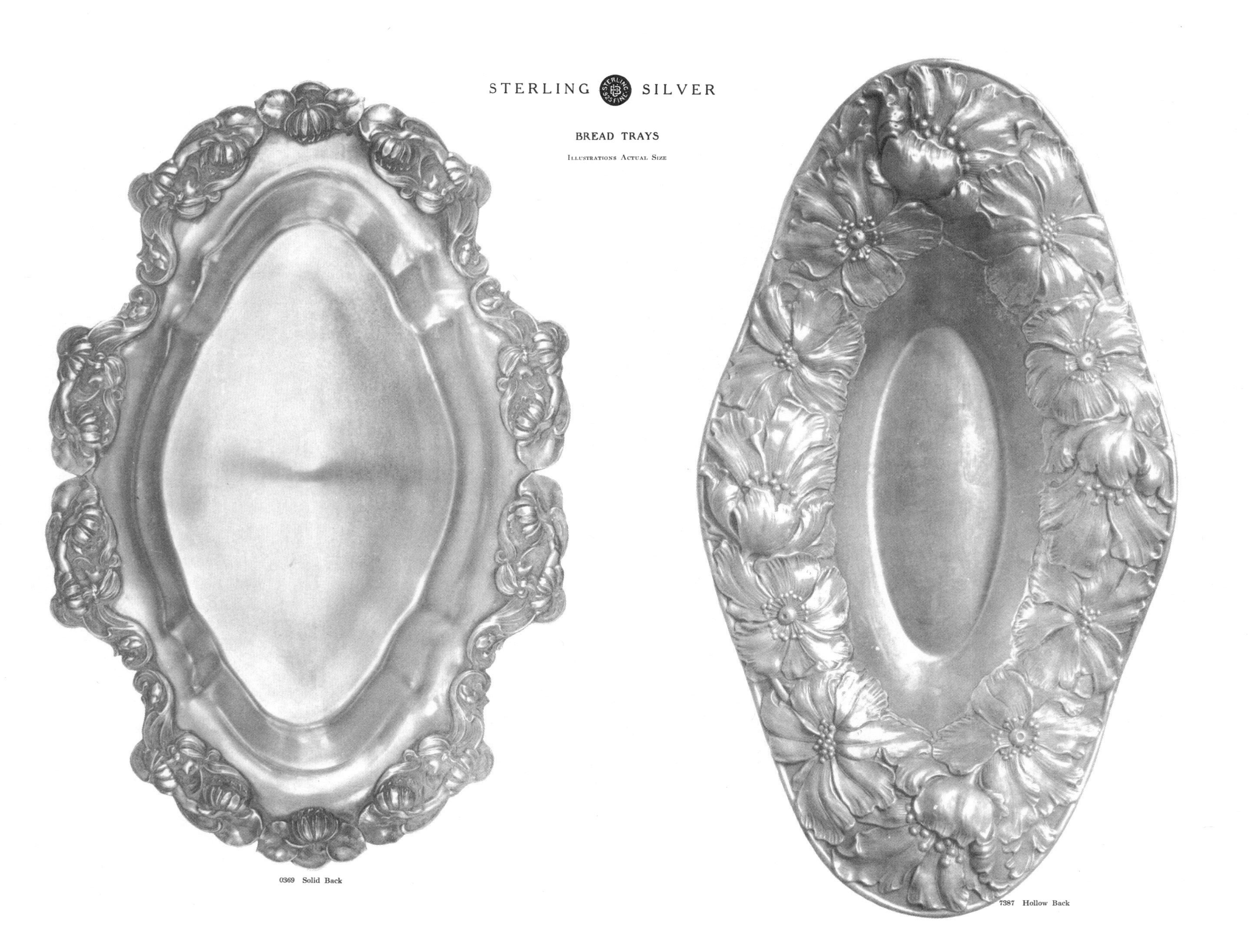

0369 Solid Back

7387 Hollow Back

STERLING SILVER

TRAYS

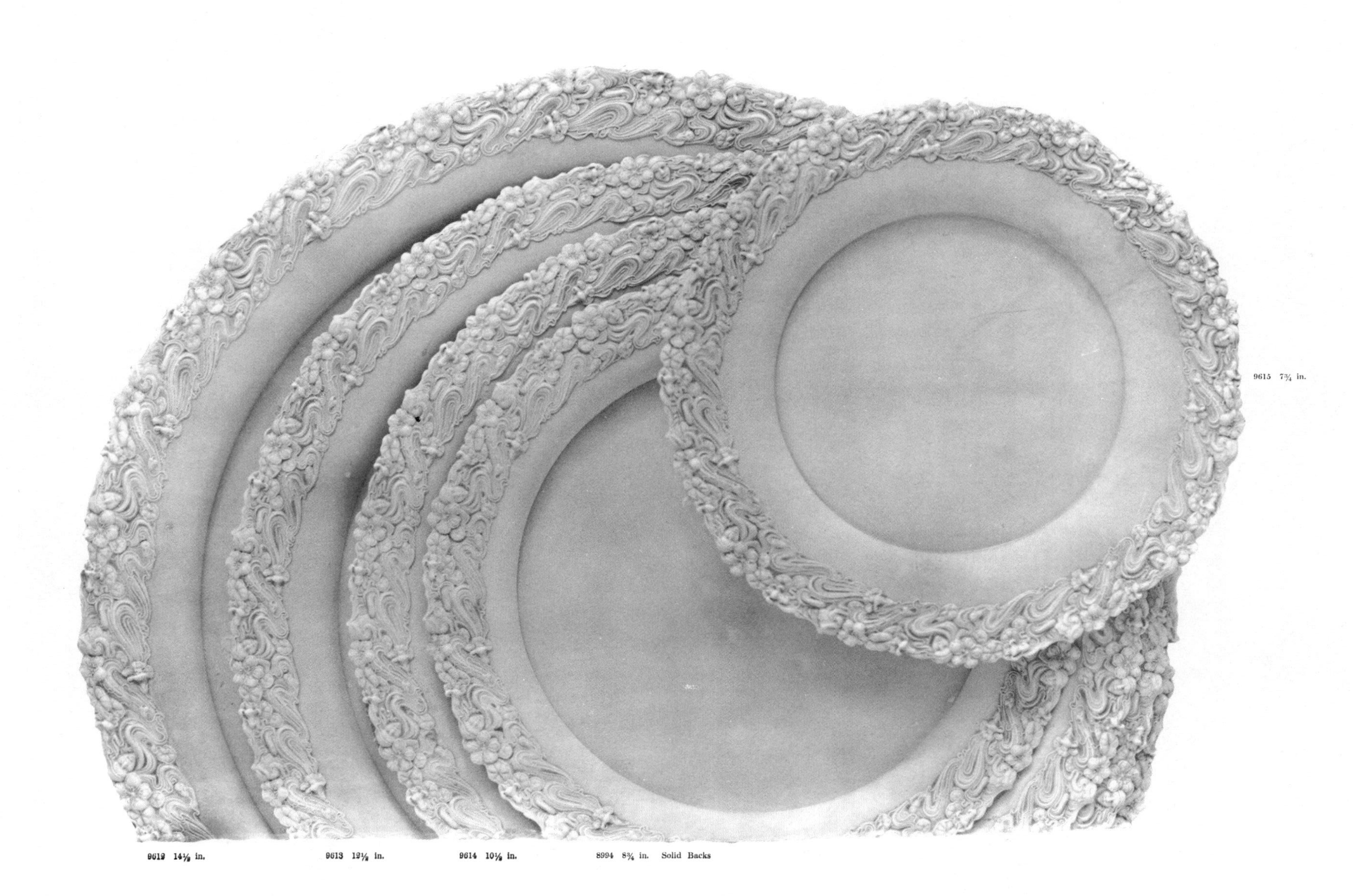

9615 7¾ in.

9612 14⅛ in. 9613 12⅛ in. 9614 10⅛ in. 8994 8¾ in. Solid Backs

STERLING SILVER

COMB AND BRUSH TRAYS

Illustrations Actual Size

0538 Solid Backs 0540

STERLING  SILVER

COMPORTS

Illustrations Actual Size

0354

0354 Side View

Solid Backs

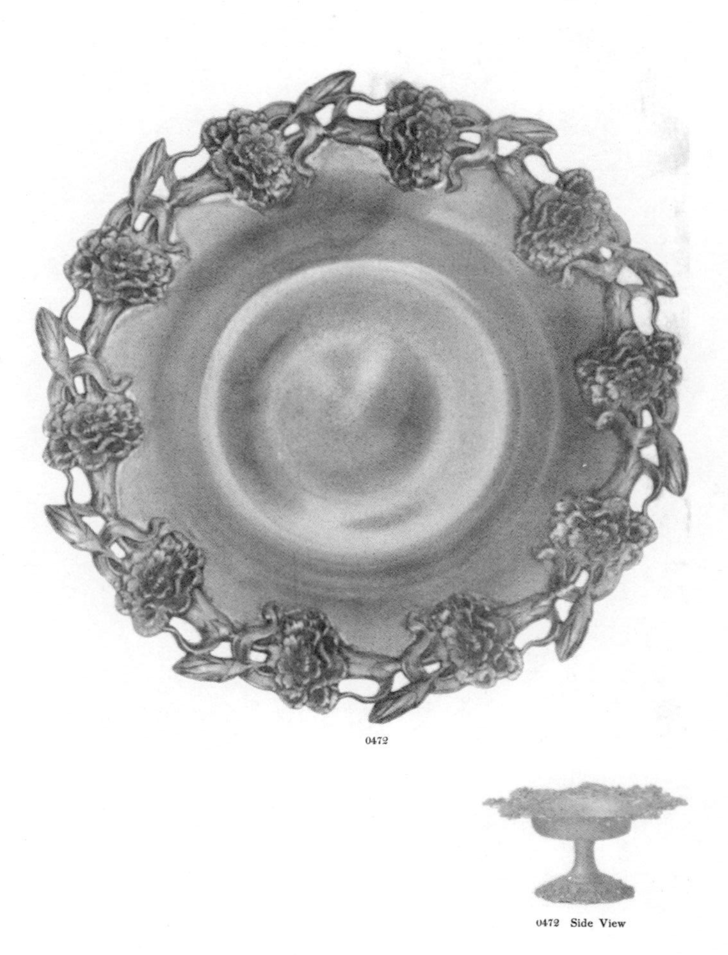

0472

0472 Side View

STERLING  SILVER

COMPORTS

Illustrations Actual Size

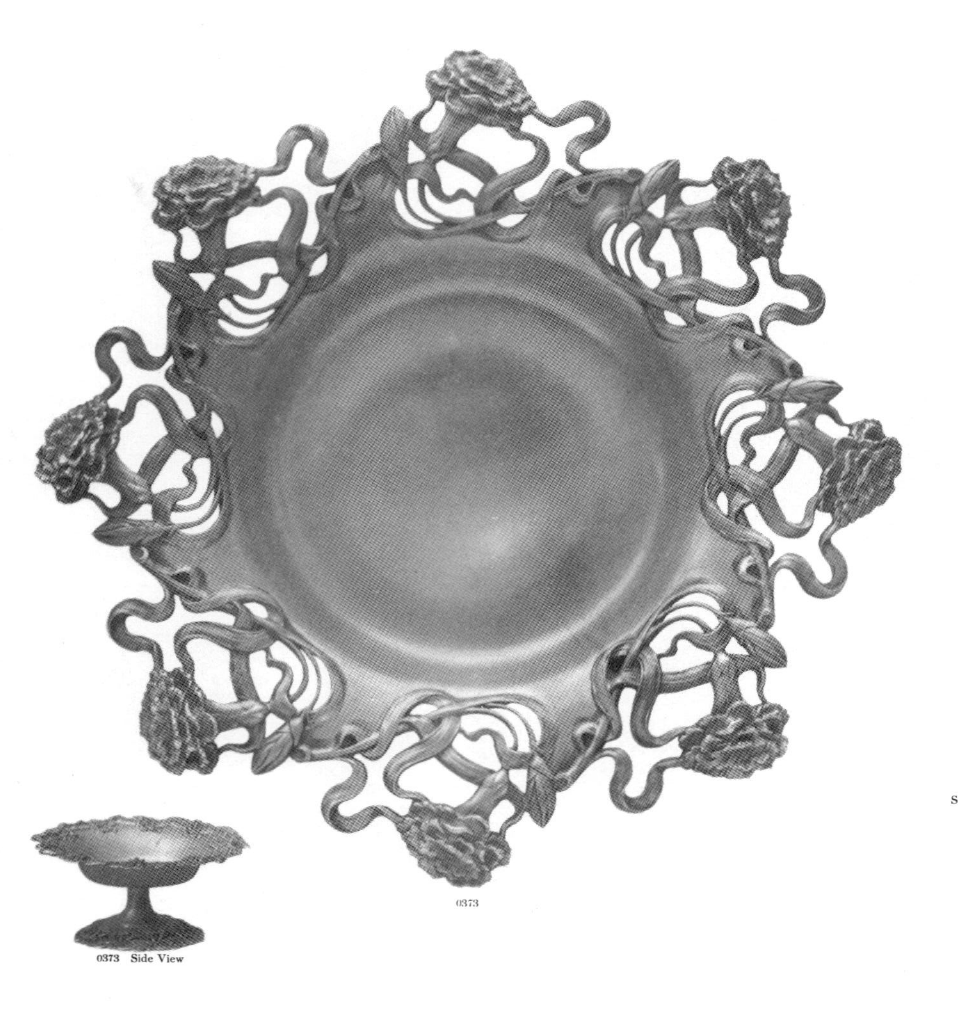

0373

0373 Side View

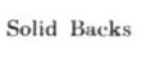

Solid Backs

0332

0332 Side View

BUTTER DISHES

Illustrations Actual Size

0384

0380

0378

0766

Solid Backs

0785

Illustrations Actual Size

0513 Wine Coaster

0524 Wine Coaster

0341 Gravy Boat
0505 Gravy Boat, Medium
0506 Gravy Boat, Large

0787 Tankard; Height, 6⅛ inches; Capacity, 2¾ pints.
02517 Tankard; Plain; Height, 6⅛ inches; Capacity, 2¾ pints.
02516 Tankard; Plain; Height, 5⅞ inches; Capacity, 2 pints.
02515 Tankard; Plain; Height, 5⅛ inches; Capacity, 1¾ pints.

0342 Gravy Boat Tray
0699 Gravy Boat Tray, Medium
0507 Gravy Boat Tray, Large

BON BON DISHES

Illustrations Actual Size

0859

0933 Solid Backs

BON-BON DISHES

Illustrations Actual Size

0858

0855

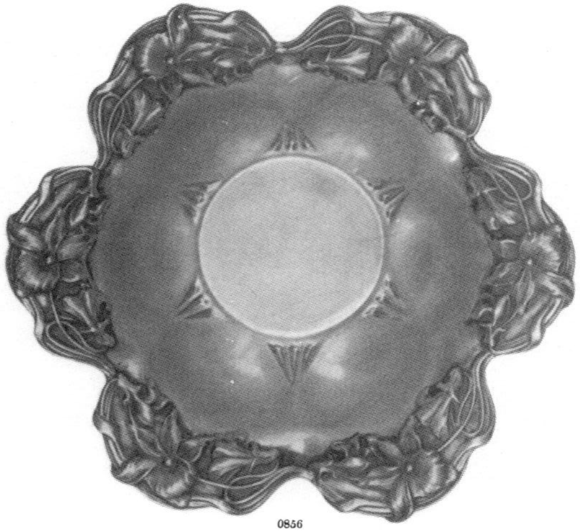

0856

0850

Solid Backs

0854

BON BON TRAYS

ILLUSTRATIONS ACTUAL SIZE

9831
9831½

0394
0394½

0547
0547½

0256
0256½

8080
Ash Tray

0393
0393½

½ numbers represent Antique finish

STERLING SILVER

TRAYS

Illustrations Actual Size

0542
0542½

0153
0153½

034
034½

9604
9604½

8597
8597½

0155
0155½

½ numbers represent Antique finish

ASH TRAYS

ILLUSTRATIONS ACTUAL SIZE

0554
0554½

0395
0395½

0543
0543½

9830
9830½

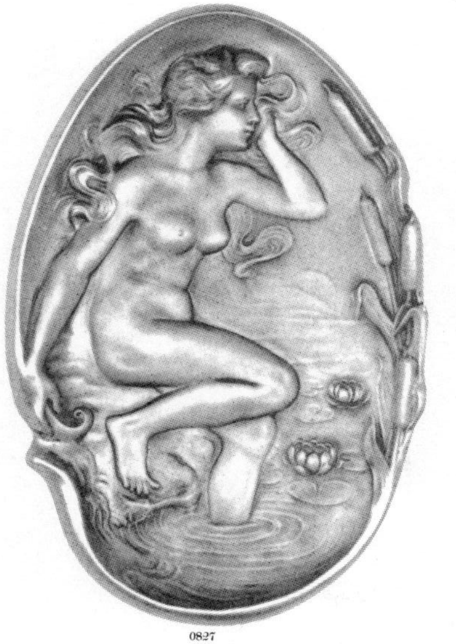

0827
0827½

0549
0549½

0154
0154½

½ numbers represent Antique finish

STERLING SILVER

ASH TRAYS

Illustrations Actual Size

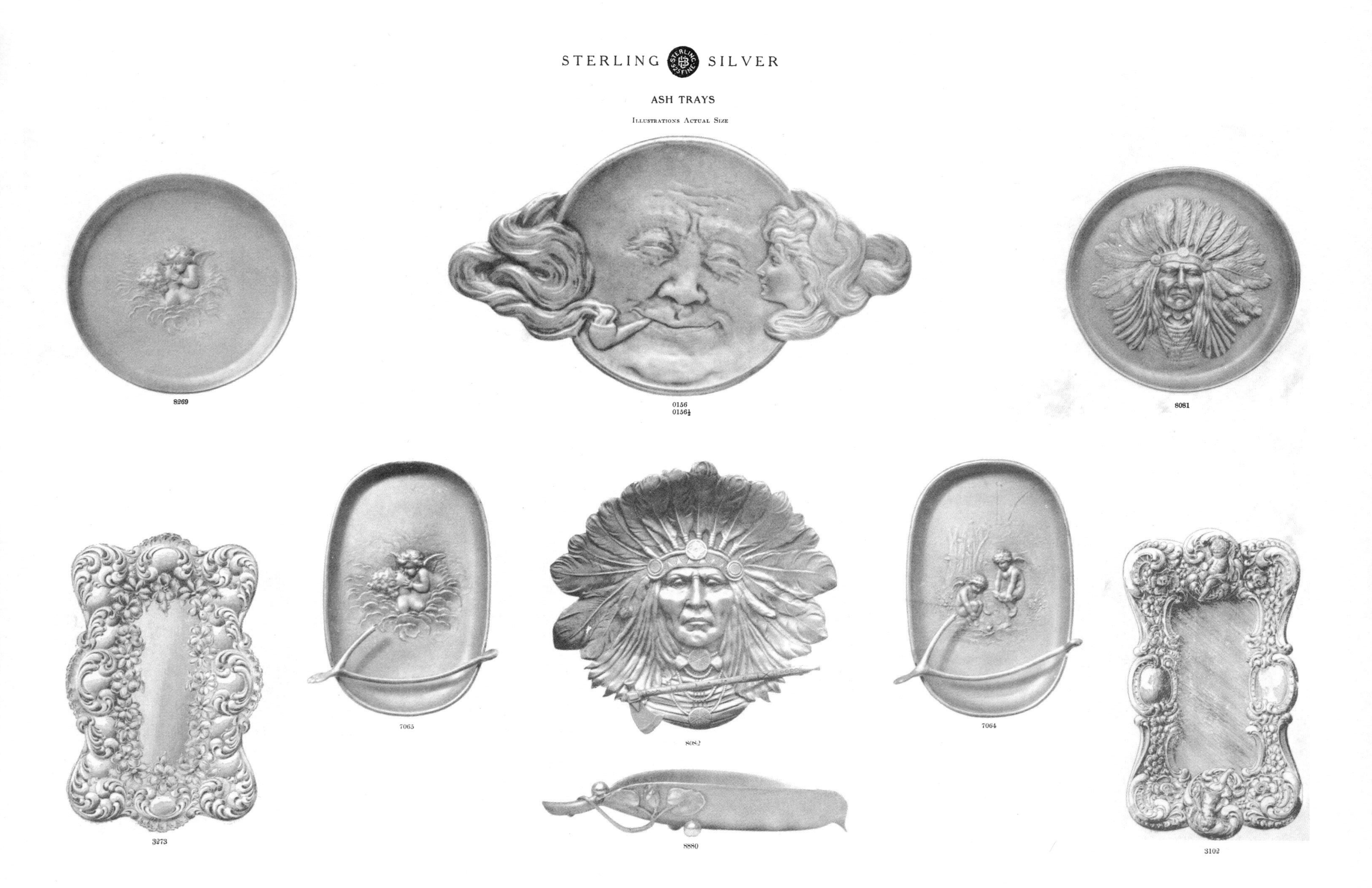

PIN AND ASH TRAYS

Illustrations Actual Size

8630
8630½

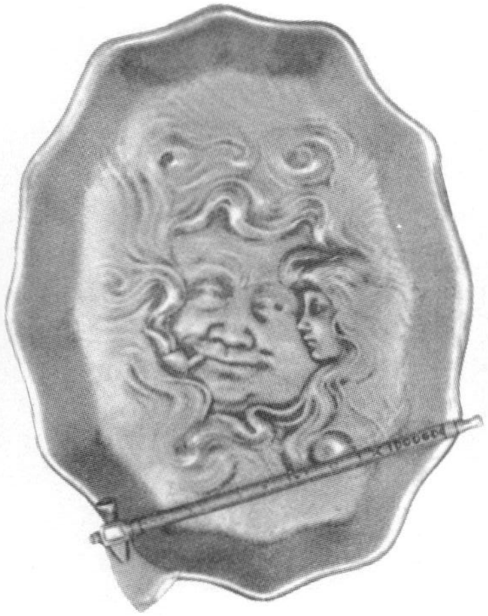

0990
0990½

0157
0157½

9941
9941½

8629
8629½

9940

0531
0531½

0826
0826½

9939
9939½

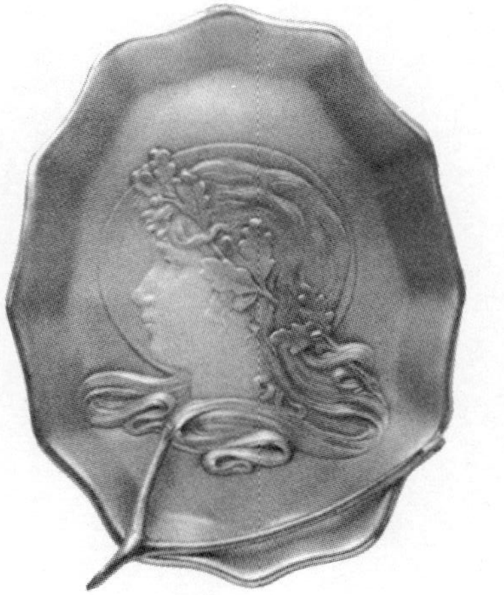

9942
9942½

½ numbers represent Antique finish

STERLING  SILVER

JEWEL CASES

ILLUSTRATIONS ACTUAL SIZE

037

8803

8806

0736

8805

All Jewel Cases Lined

0735

STERLING SILVER

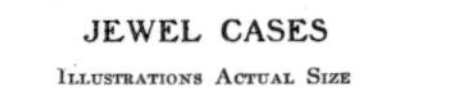

JEWEL CASES

Illustrations Actual Size

8807

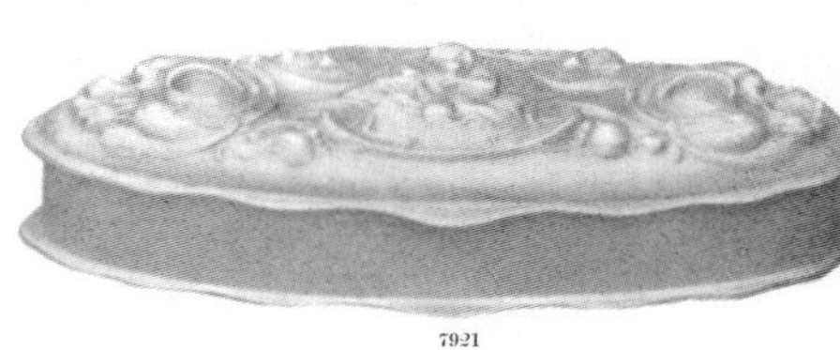
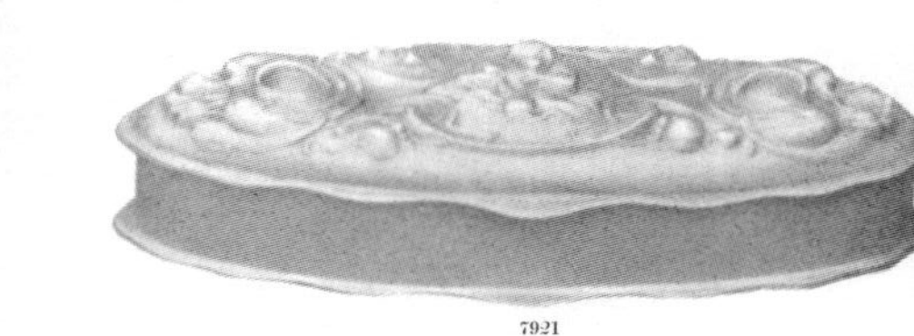
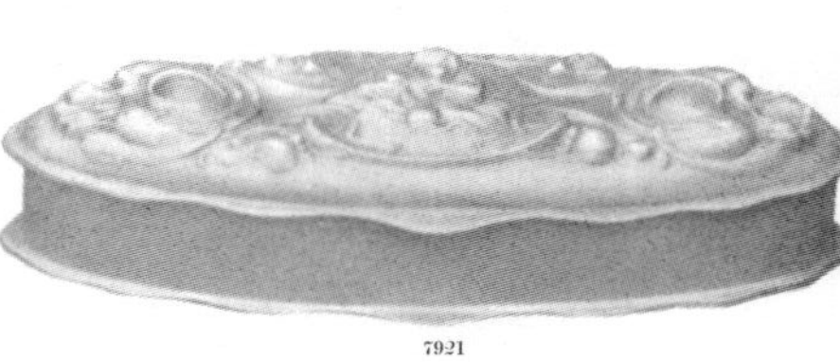
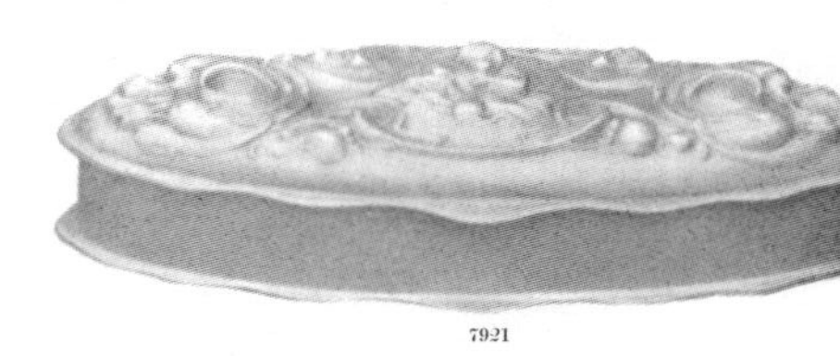

7921

9790

036

8808

All Jewel Cases Lined

8804

STERLING SILVER

PIN CUSHIONS AND JEWEL CASES

ILLUSTRATIONS ACTUAL SIZE

7923

9665

01175

9664

9660
9791 Size Smaller

9662

9661

9663

CANDLE STICKS

Illustrations Actual Size

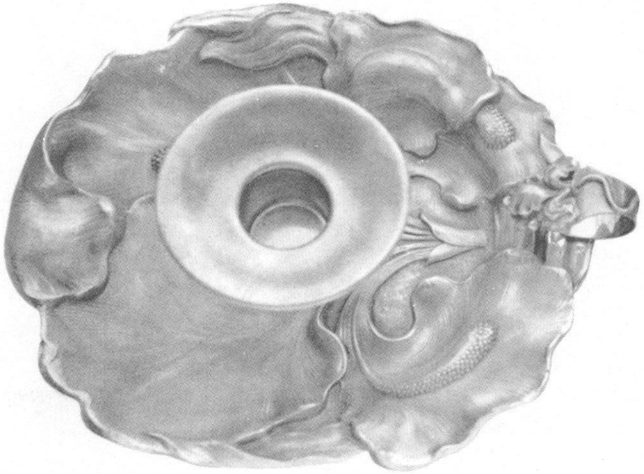

0719

7275

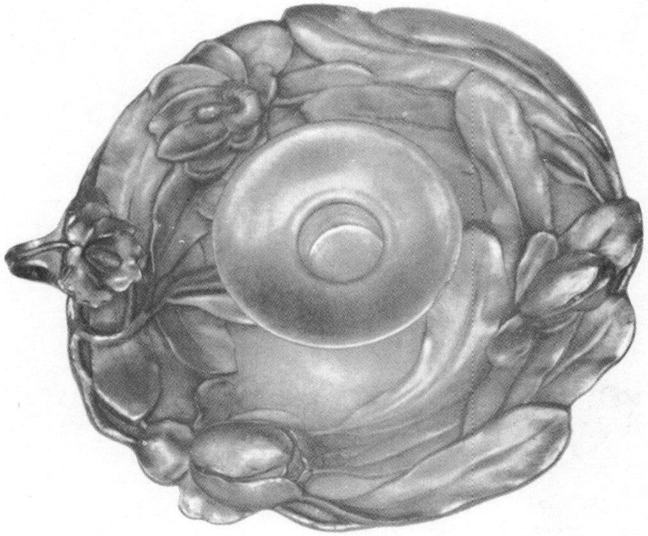

0604

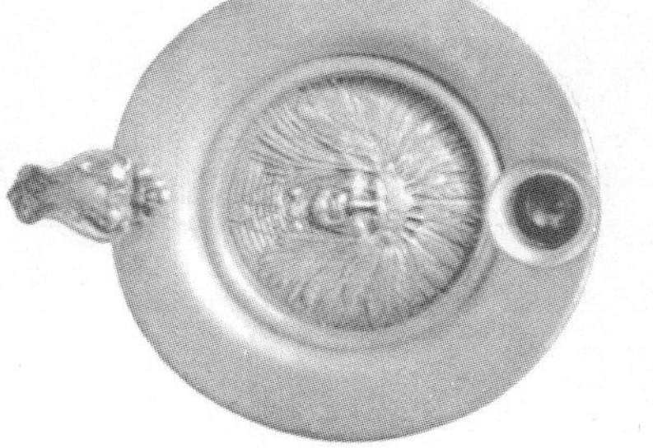

9963

7725

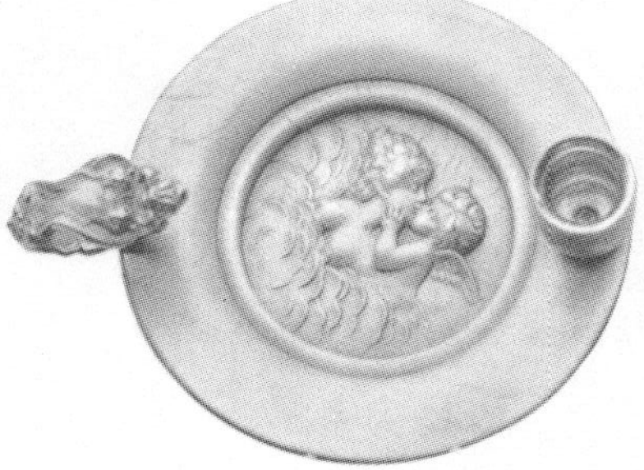

9553

CHEESE HOLDERS AND MUSTARD CUPS

Illustrations Actual Size

0102

0101

MAC LAREN'S IMPERIAL CHEESE

For Large Size Holders

0100

0104

098

095

097

099

MAC LAREN'S IMPERIAL CHEESE

For Small Size Holders

02055

096

0103

0775

02056

STERLING SILVER

TABASCO SAUCE AND LISTERINE HOLDERS

Illustrations Actual Size

TABASCO SAUCE HOLDERRS

0770 0771 0769 0768 0767 01131

0774 01134 0773 0772 01133

LISTERINE HOLDERS

094 092 090 091 093 01132

STERLING SILVER

SHAVING BRUSHES

0996

0997

0931

0691

033

0584

031

0717

9644

9645

7918 Folding
7919 Non-separable

8282

0210 Folding

032

9647

6963 Folding

0690

9646

8881

3099

2609

STERLING SILVER

RAZOR STROPS, SHAVING MUGS AND SOAP BOXES

Illustrations Actual Size

STERLING SILVER

NAPKIN RINGS

ILLUSTRATIONS ACTUAL SIZE

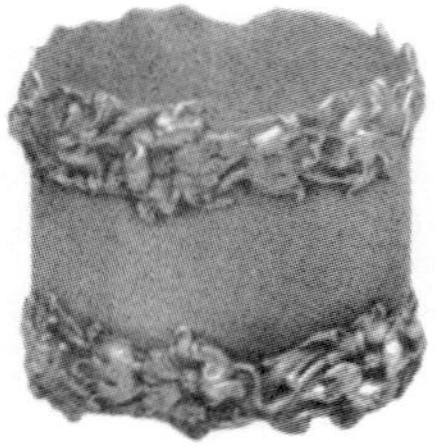

0811  0815  0814  0812  0813

0817  0822  0816  0820

0819  0846 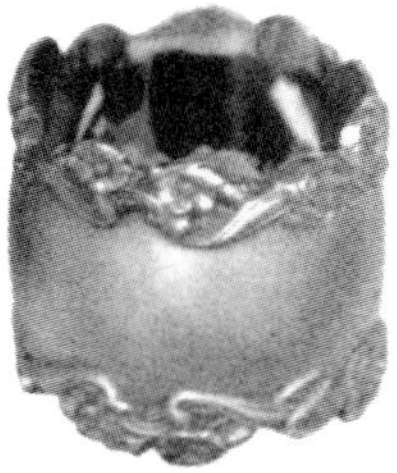 0821  0818

7260  6535

NAPKIN HOLDER
9910

7259  9826

UMBRELLA HANDLES

Illustrations Actual Size

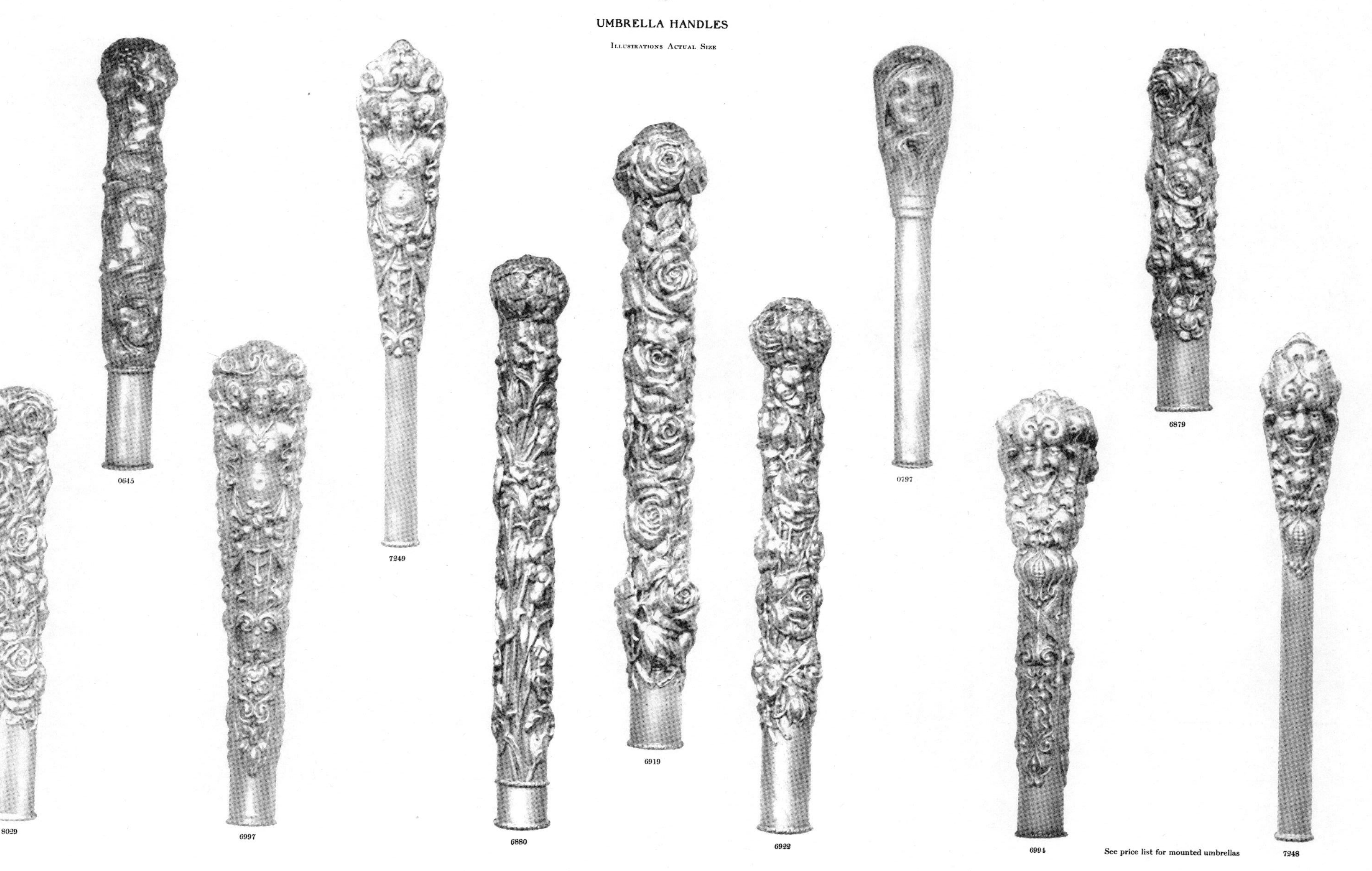

See price list for mounted umbrellas

STERLING SILVER

UMBRELLA HANDLES

Illustrations Actual Size

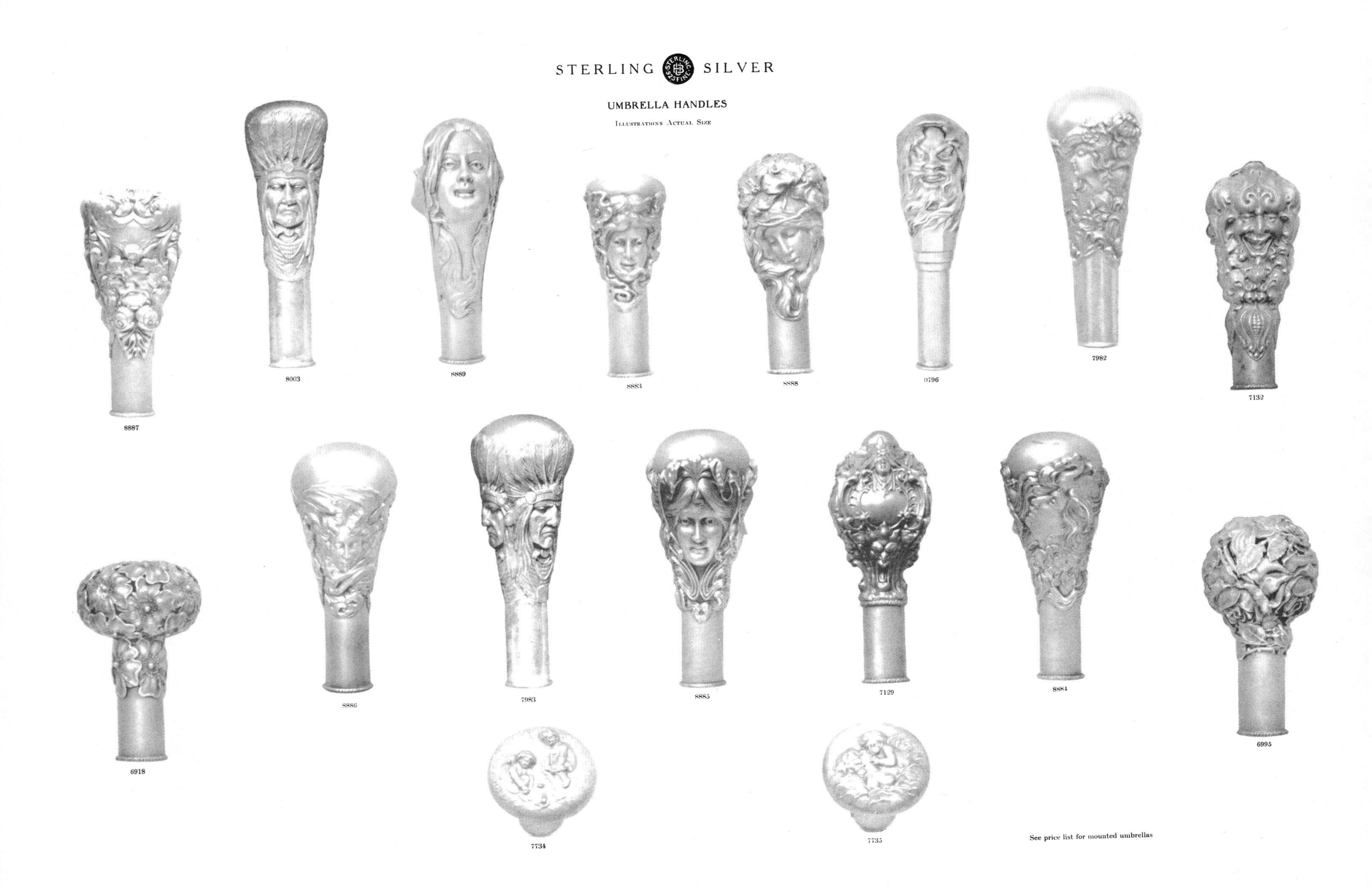

See price list for mounted umbrellas

STERLING  SILVER

FLASKS

Illustrations Actual Size

7073
8279 Indian

0983

Capacity one-half pint

8550

7071

4038

7072

7066

3492

FLASKS

ILLUSTRATIONS ACTUAL SIZE

6489 Alligator

0694
0695 Bath

6244

6166
6163 Steeplechase

0992 Alligator

3193
3390 Bayonet Top

2362

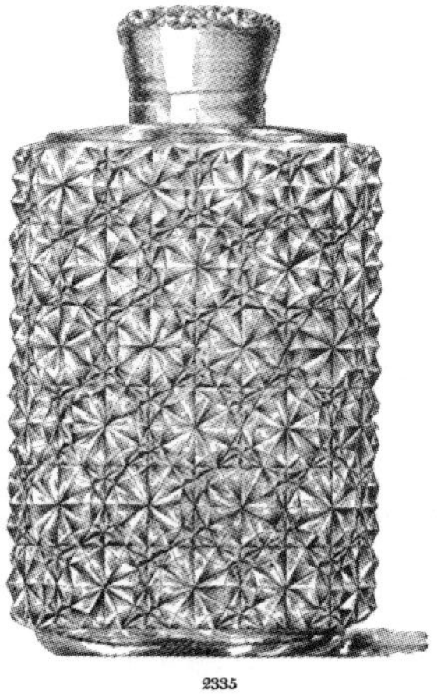

2335

0693

2253

STERLING SILVER

CIGARETTE CASES

Illustrations Actual Size

8548 · 6780 · 6989 · 6782 · 8264

01710 · 7036 · 8540 · 7030 · 6783

6655 · 0546 · 0986 · 8537 · 8255 · 6657

STERLING SILVER

CIGARETTE CASES

Illustrations Actual Size

2311 Single Row
2424 Double Row

7018 Single Row
7027 Double Row

8546 Single Row
8547 Double Row

8334 Single Row
8192 Double Row

8538 Single Row
8539 Double Row

5992 Single Row
5993 Double Row

0987 Single Row
0988 Double Row

7012 Single Row
7021 Double Row

8542 Single Row
8543 Double Row

7016 Single Row
6955 Double Row

7017 Single Row
7026 Double Row

7010 Single Row
7019 Double Row

2442 Single Row
5388 Double Row

8545

7009

7008

9666 Cigar Case

8541

7003

7001

MATCH BOXES AND HOLDERS

Illustrations Actual Size

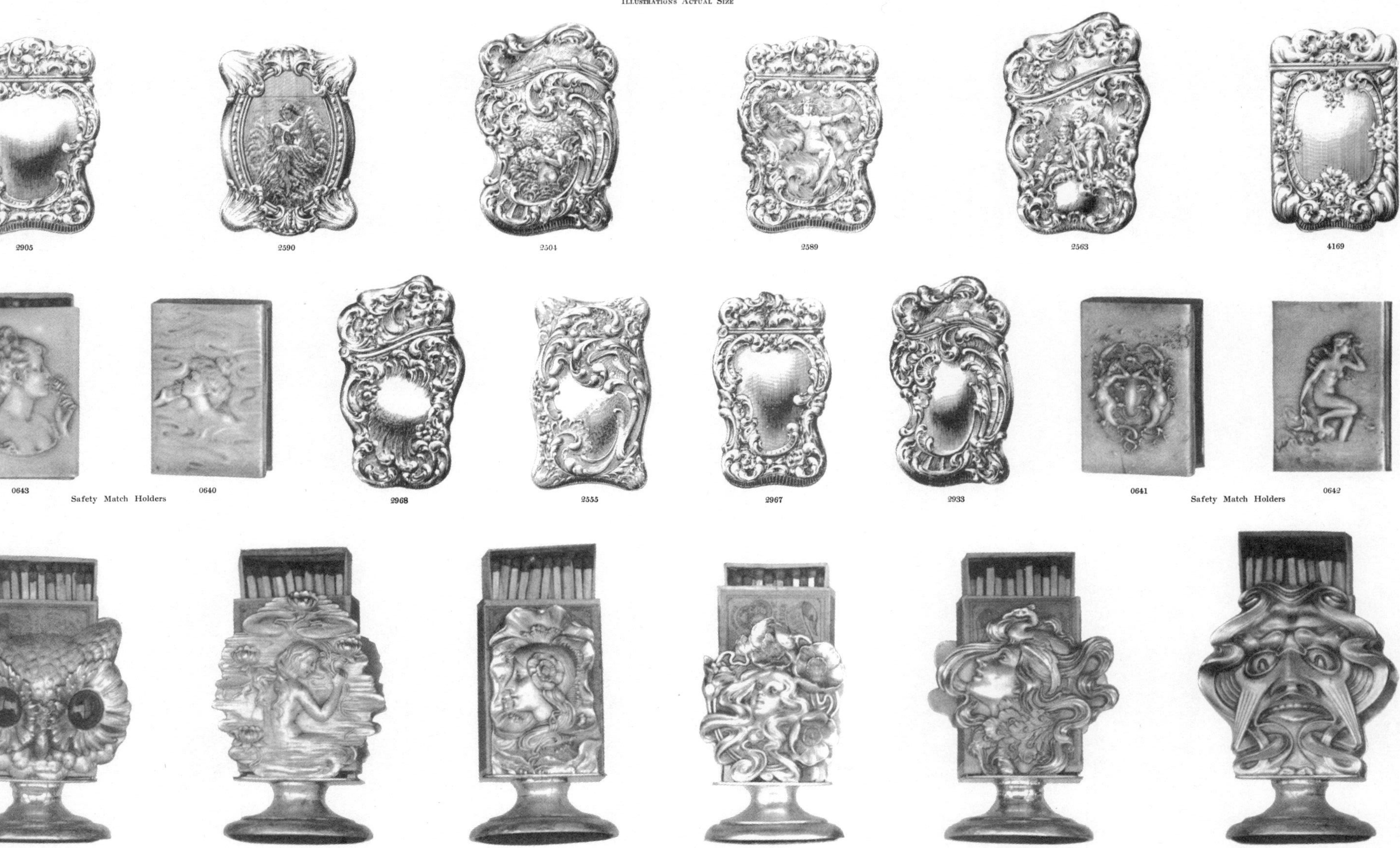

2905 2590 2504 2589 2563 4169

0643 0640 Safety Match Holders 2968 2555 2967 2933 0641 0642 Safety Match Holders

0780 0778 0776 0689 0777 0779

STERLING SILVER

MATCH BOXES

Illustrations Actual Size

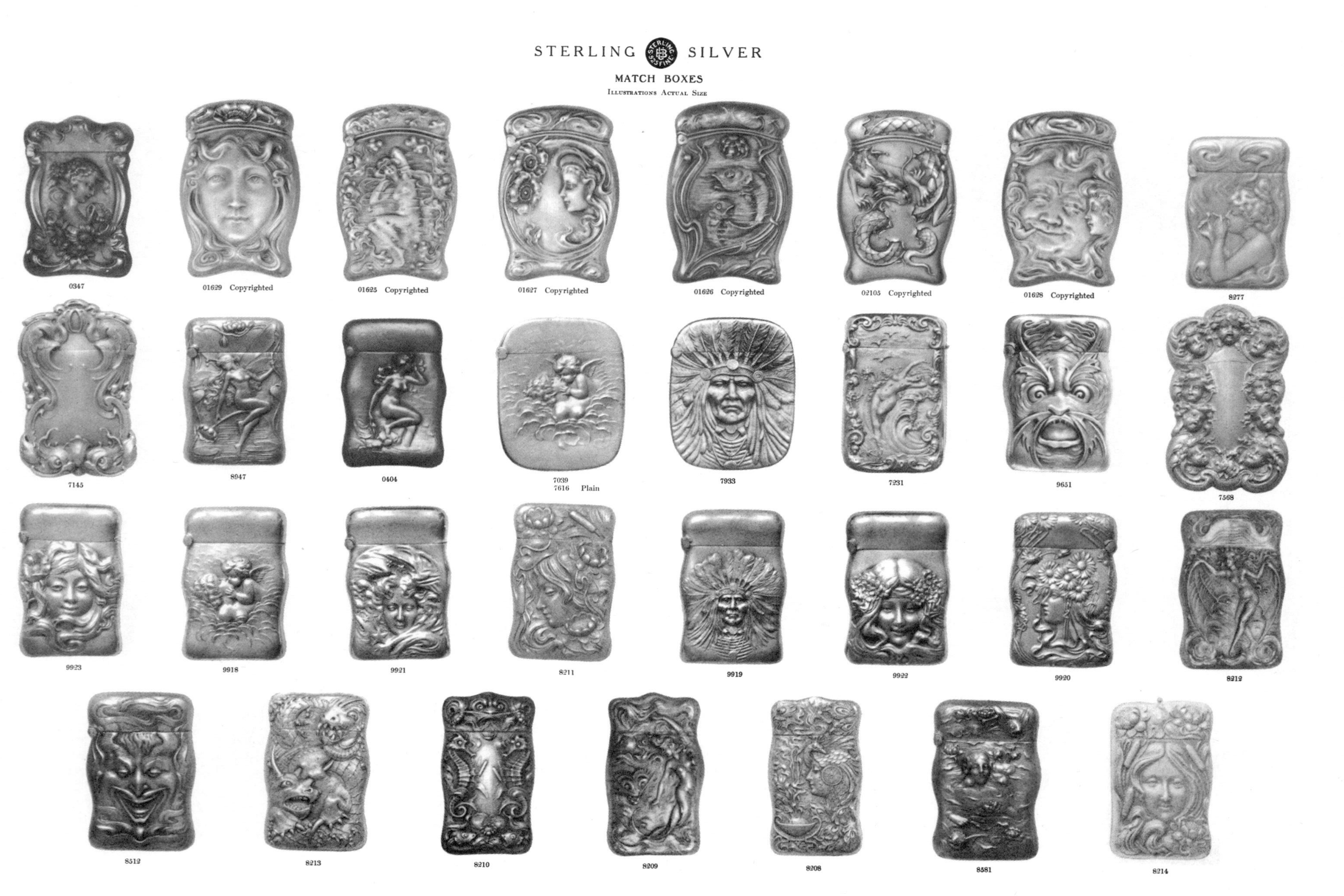

STERLING SILVER

LOVE'S DREAM DESK SET

ILLUSTRATIONS HALF SIZE

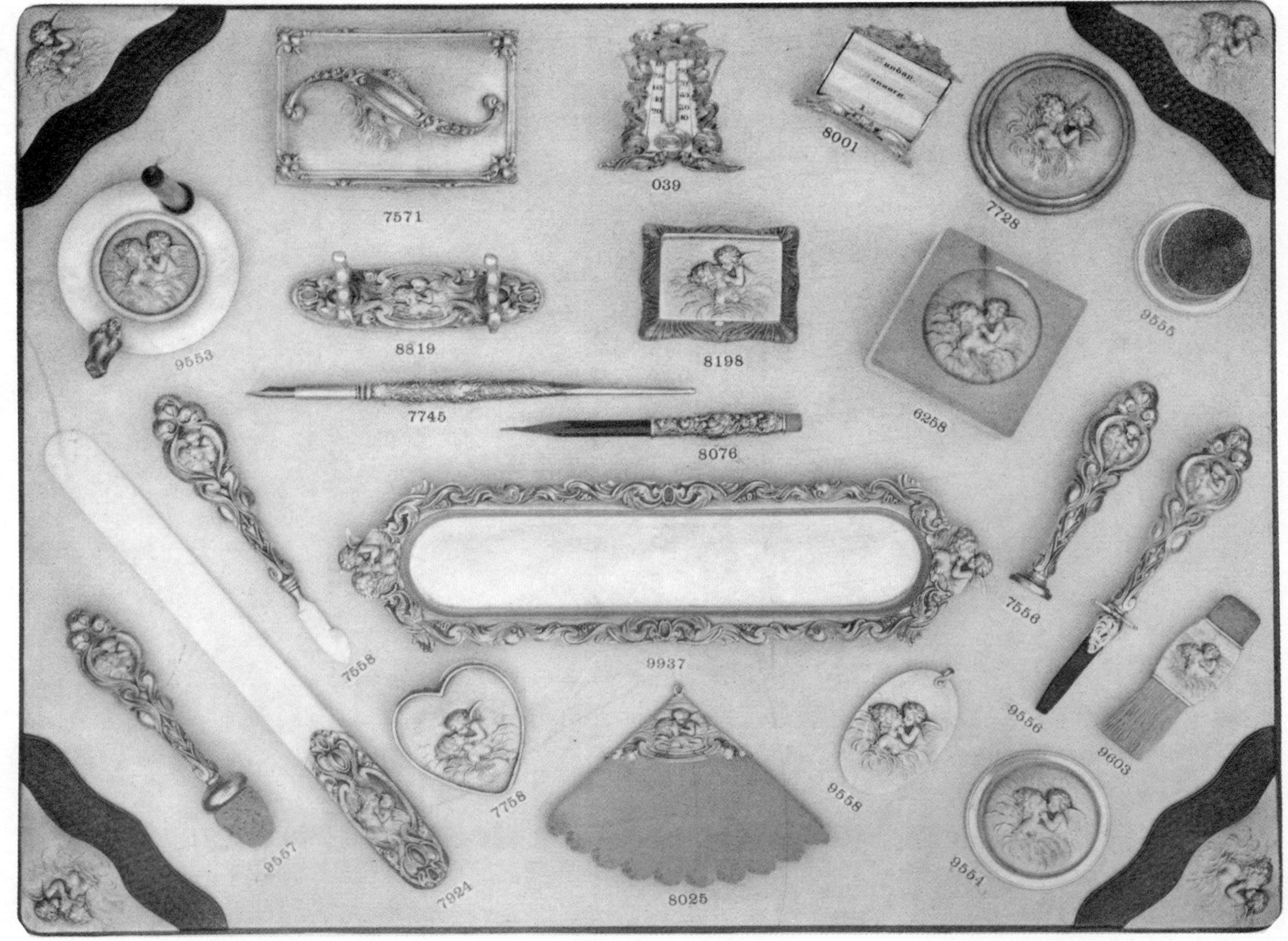

Desk Pad 16x21 inches

DESK ARTICLES

ILLUSTRATIONS ACTUAL SIZE

PEN TRAYS

ERASERS

0692

9968

9603

9964

ERASERS

7759

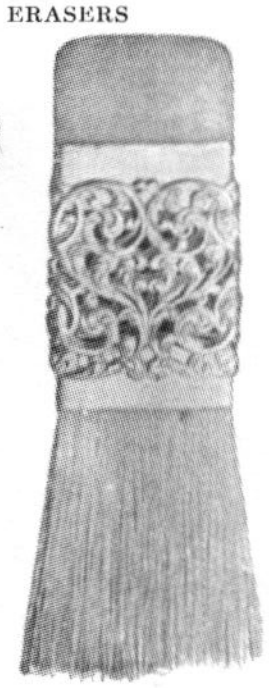

9856

332

LETTER CLIPS

8180

8818

0392

0556 Love's Dream Center
0557 Chilly Cupid Center
0558 Indian Center
0605 Evangeline Center
0606 He Loves Me Center
0607 Dawn Center

LETTER CLIPS

01943

01210

7283

7757

7680 Letter File

9937

9972 Letter File

STERLING SILVER

THERMOMETERS AND BLOTTERS

ILLUSTRATIONS ACTUAL SIZE

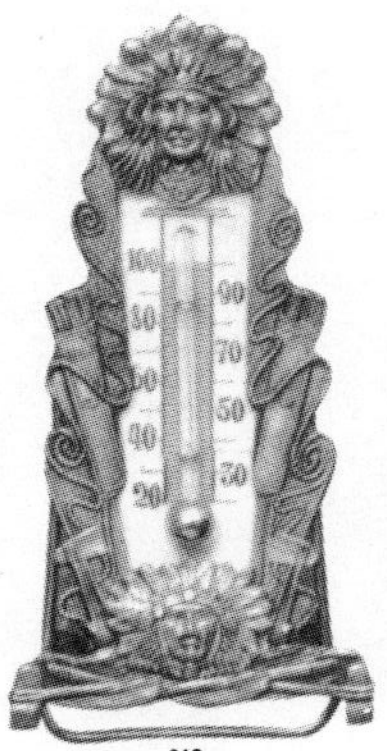

042

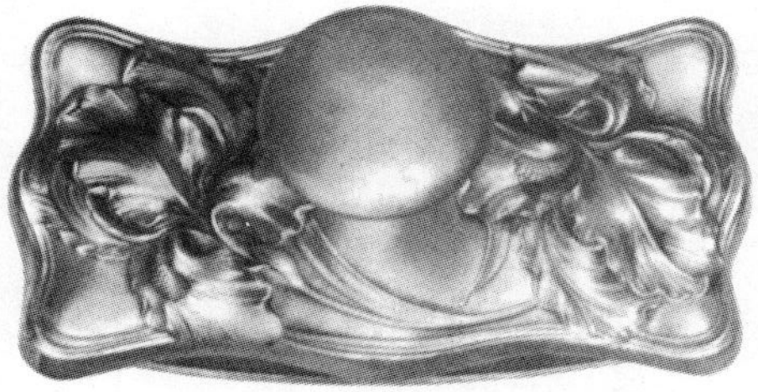

0739

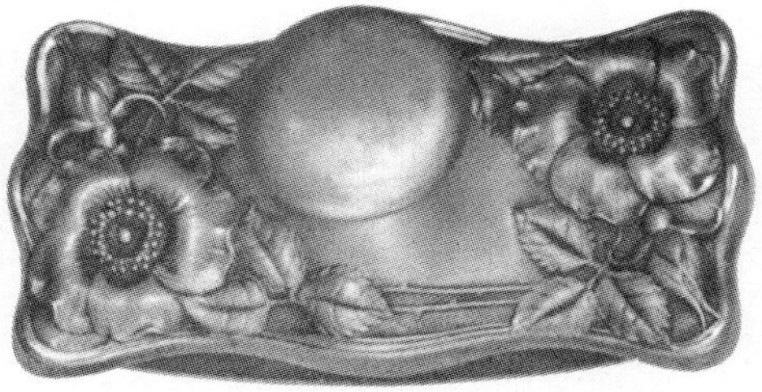

0740

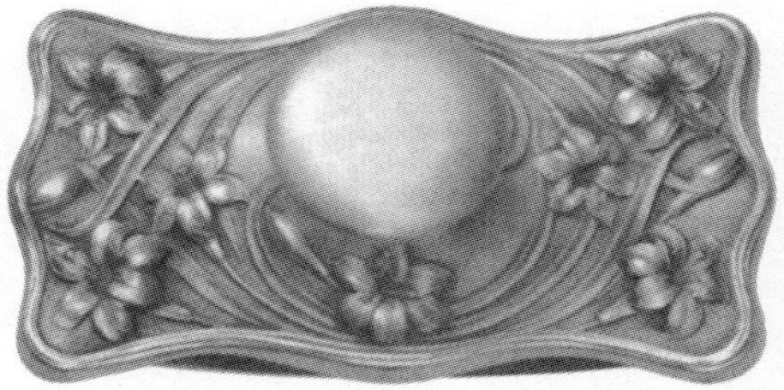

0741

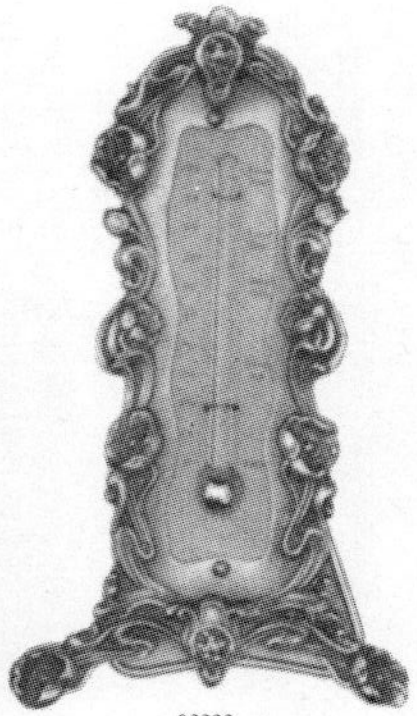

02222

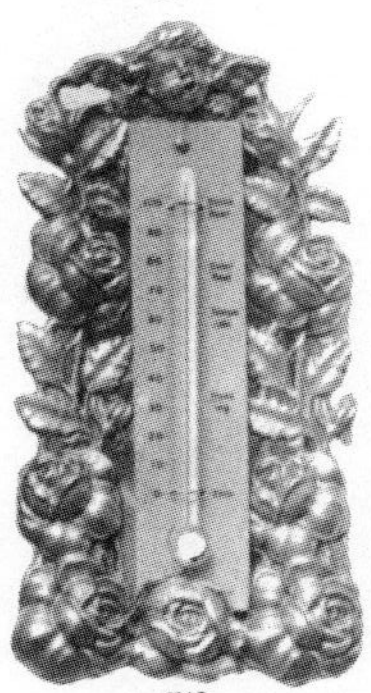

6953

7571 With Handle
7192 Without Handle

01135

7573 With Handle
7195 Without Handle

02221

039

4138

7736

3307

02220

STERLING SILVER

DESK ARTICLES

ILLUSTRATIONS ACTUAL SIZE

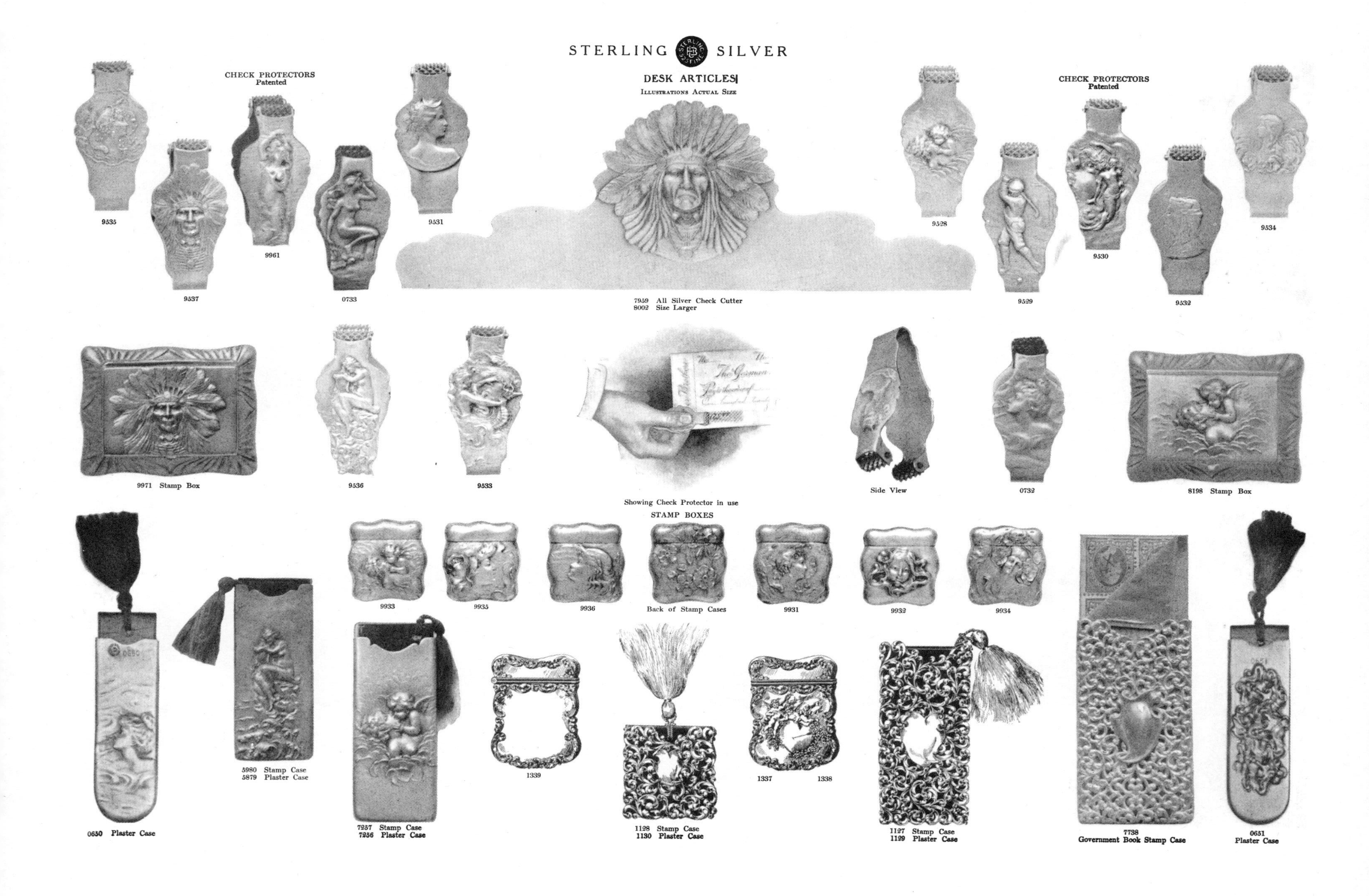

CHECK PROTECTORS
Patented

9535

9537

9961

0733

9531

7959 All Silver Check Cutter
8002 Size Larger

CHECK PROTECTORS
Patented

9528

9529

9530

9532

9534

9971 Stamp Box

9536

9533

Showing Check Protector in use

Side View

0732

8198 Stamp Box

STAMP BOXES

9933

9935

9936

Back of Stamp Cases

9931

9932

9934

0650 Plaster Case

5980 Stamp Case
5879 Plaster Case

7257 Stamp Case
7256 Plaster Case

1339

1128 Stamp Case
1130 Plaster Case

1337

1338

1127 Stamp Case
1129 Plaster Case

7738
Government Book Stamp Case

0651
Plaster Case

DESK ARTICLES

Illustrations Actual Size

PEN HOLDERS

01599

7746

7747

7744

0710 Ink Stand

PEN HOLDERS

7743

7742

7745

195

01113 Patent Ink Well with Top

Top for 01113

0781 Patent Ink Well without Top

PEN RACKS

0700 Evangeline
0705 Reine des Fleurs

0715 Pen Box

0782 Patent Ink Well without Top

Top for 01114

01114 Patent Ink Well with Top

8819

0702 He Loves Me
0704 Peep o' Day

PEN RACKS

0701 Dawn
0703 Les Secrete

8870

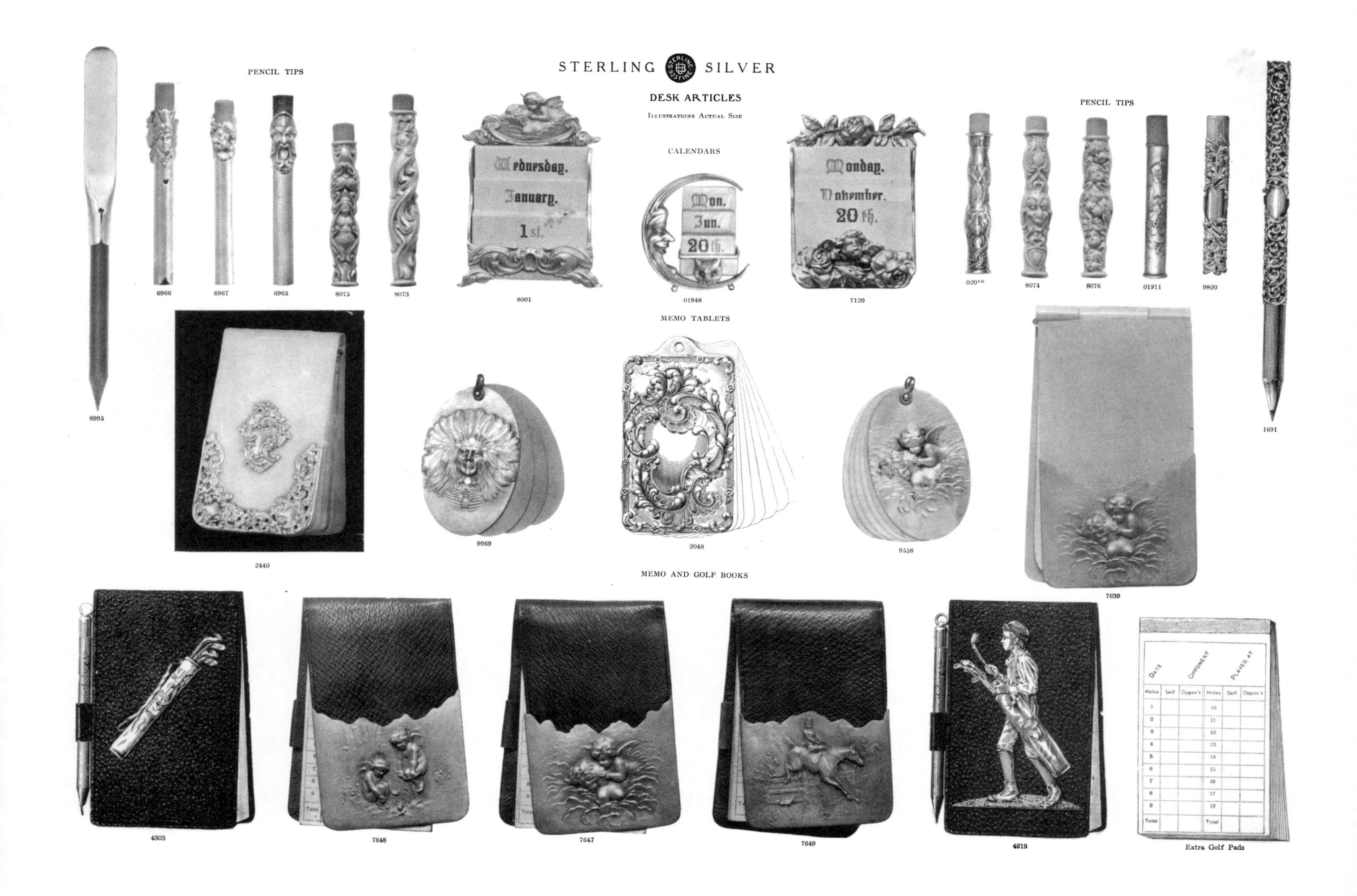
STERLING SILVER
DESK ARTICLES
Illustrations Actual Size
PENCIL TIPS
8995
6966
6967
6965
8075
8073
8001
CALENDARS
01948
7120
PENCIL TIPS
0201
8074
8076
01911
9820
1691
MEMO TABLETS
2440
9969
2048
9558
7639
MEMO AND GOLF BOOKS
4303
7648
7647
7649
4219
Date
Opponent
Played at
Holes
Self
Oppon't
Total
Extra Golf Pads

STERLING SILVER

VASES

Illustrations Actual Size

LORGNETTES

ILLUSTRATIONS ACTUAL SIZE

9955 Front and Back alike
9955½

8985 Back like 9955
8985½
9834 With Mirror
9834½

8982
Front and Back alike
8982½

8984 Back like 8982
8984½
9832 With Mirror
9832½ With Mirror

9756
Back like 8982
9756½

8983 Back like 074
8983½
9833 With Mirror
9833½

074
Front and Back alike
074½

7595
7595½

7124
7124½
6920 Without Stones
6920½

6877
6877½

6789
6789½

6739
6739½

6799
6799½

6921
6921½

6788
6788½

7741
7741½

RATTLES

Illustrations Actual Size

01930 01928 01931 01932 01929 01927

02009 02010 02011 8622 8742 8741 8740

6707 2052 8736 02008 1472 2014 2426

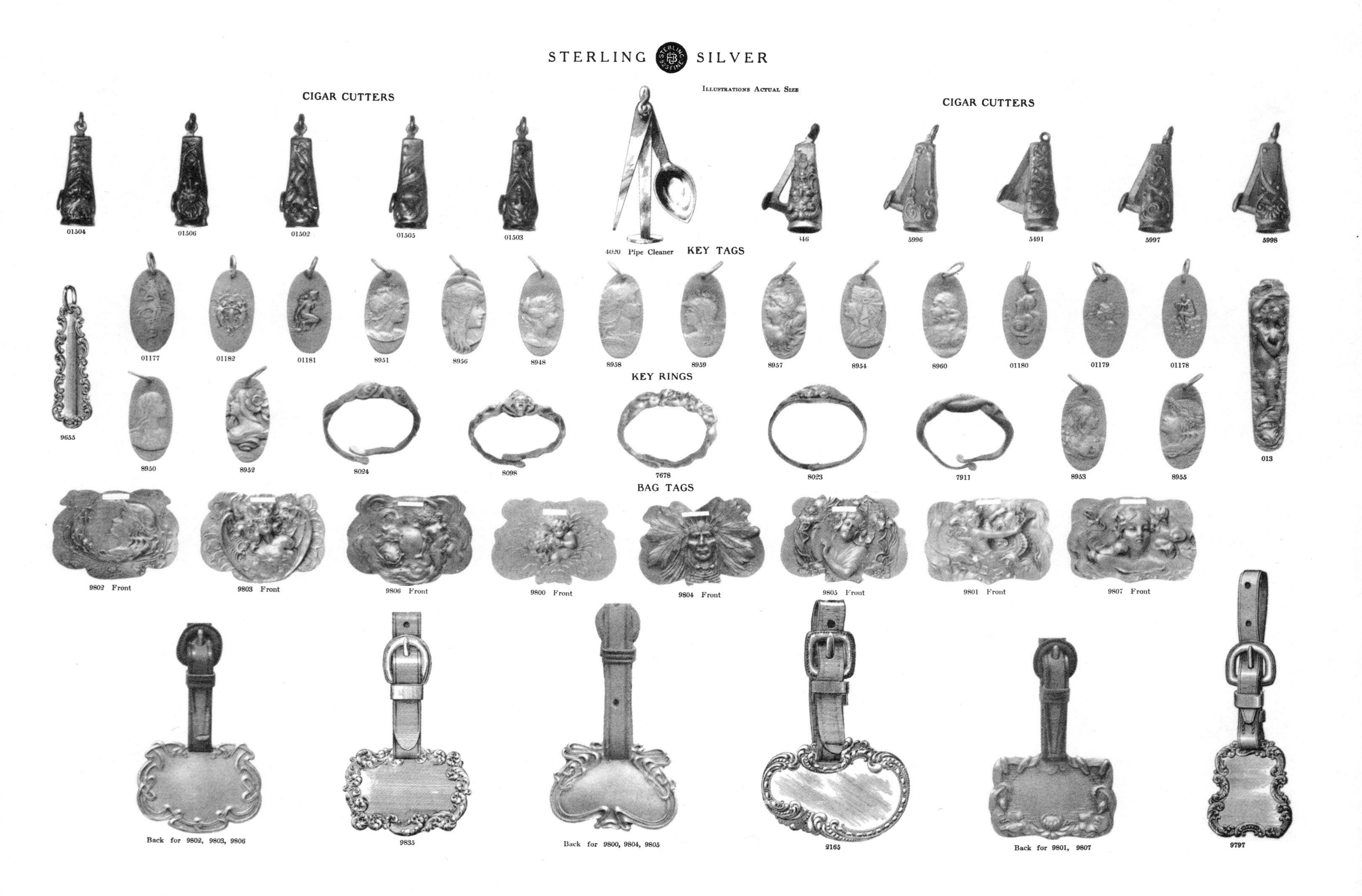
STERLING SILVER
STERLING 925 FINE
Illustrations Actual Size
CIGAR CUTTERS
01504
01506
01502
01505
01503
4020 Pipe Cleaner
CIGAR CUTTERS
346
5996
5491
5997
5998
KEY TAGS
01177
01182
01181
8951
8956
8948
8958
8959
8957
8954
8960
01180
01179
01178
9655
013
8950
8952
8953
8955
KEY RINGS
8024
8098
7678
8023
7911
BAG TAGS
9802 Front
9803 Front
9806 Front
9800 Front
9804 Front
9805 Front
9801 Front
9807 Front
Back for 9802, 9803, 9806
9835
Back for 9800, 9804, 9805
2165
Back for 9801, 9807
9797

STERLING SILVER

BOOK MARKS

Illustrations Actual Size

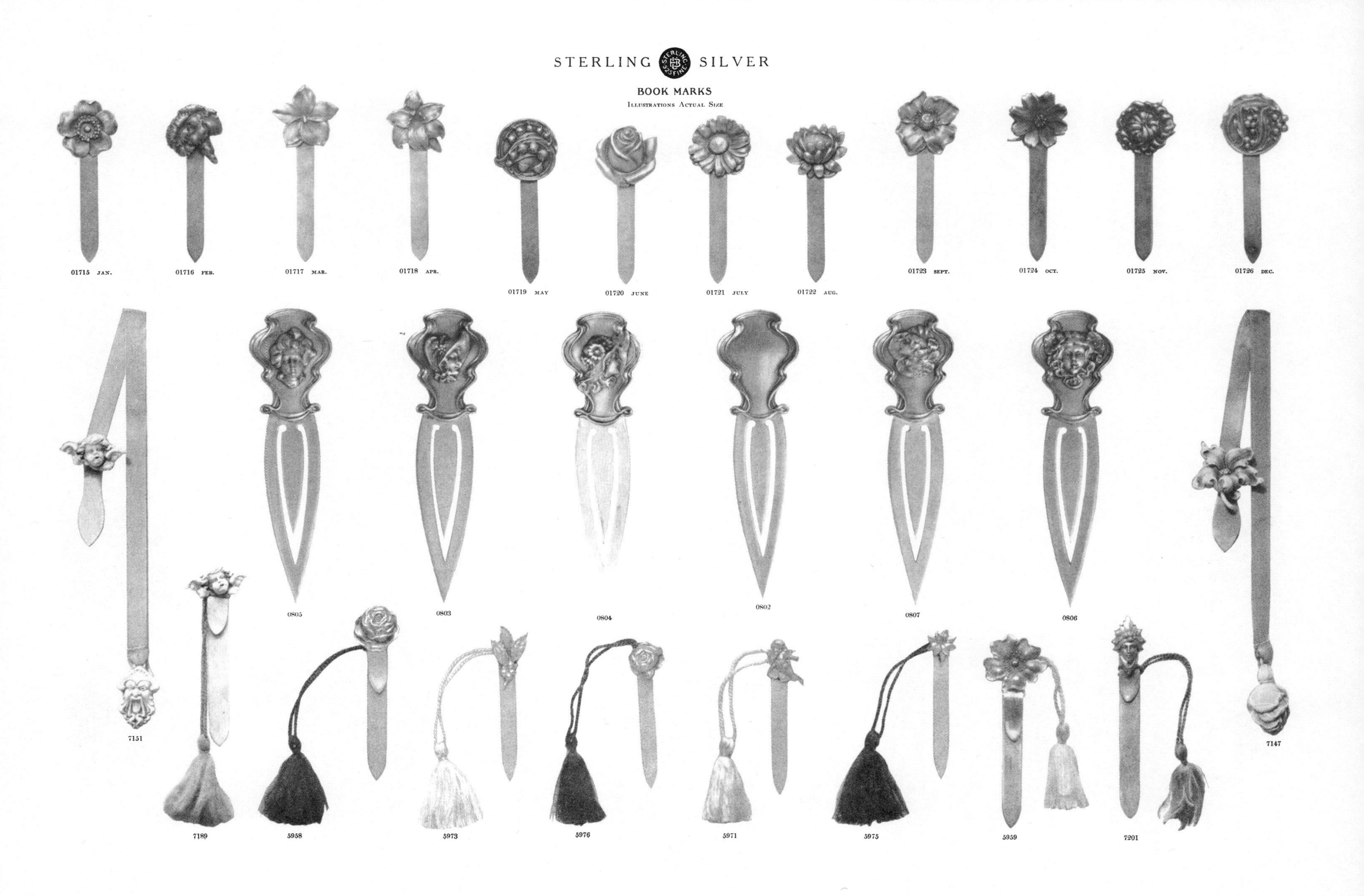

STERLING SILVER

POCKET MIRRORS AND PIN CUSHIONS

Illustrations Actual Size

7633 01167 02399 01784 9656 9658 01166

01169 9657 7634 01168 9655 9654

FLIRTATION MIRROR AND MEMO TABLET

7077 01233 01176 7076

BON BON SCOOPS

01183
7082 Love's Dawn

7756

8026

8253

01184
7083 Chilly Cupids

Illustrations Actual Size

3452 Tea Ball

4047 Tea Ball Stand

4042 Tea Strainer

7925

CURLING IRON STANDS

7393

GLOVE CLEANERS

4110

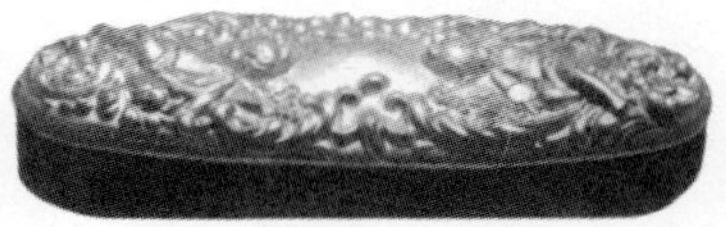

6852

6851

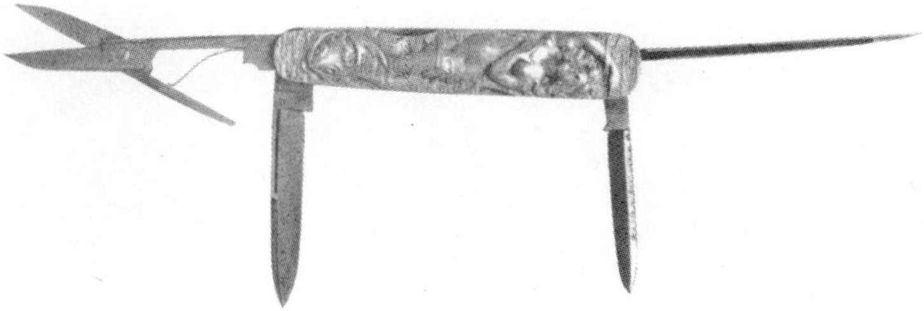

THERMOMETER CASES

1126 File Case

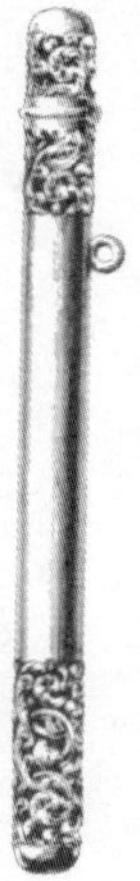

4044

1125

WHISTLES

01944

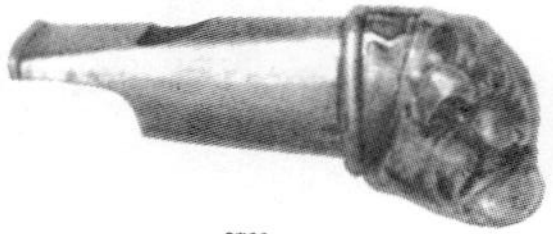

0722

01945

0721

2663

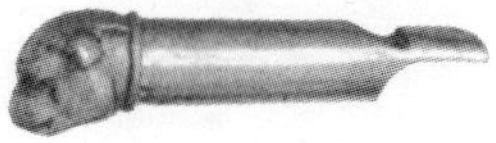

0720

9960 Pen Knife

STERLING SILVER

TAPE MEASURES

Illustrations Actual Size

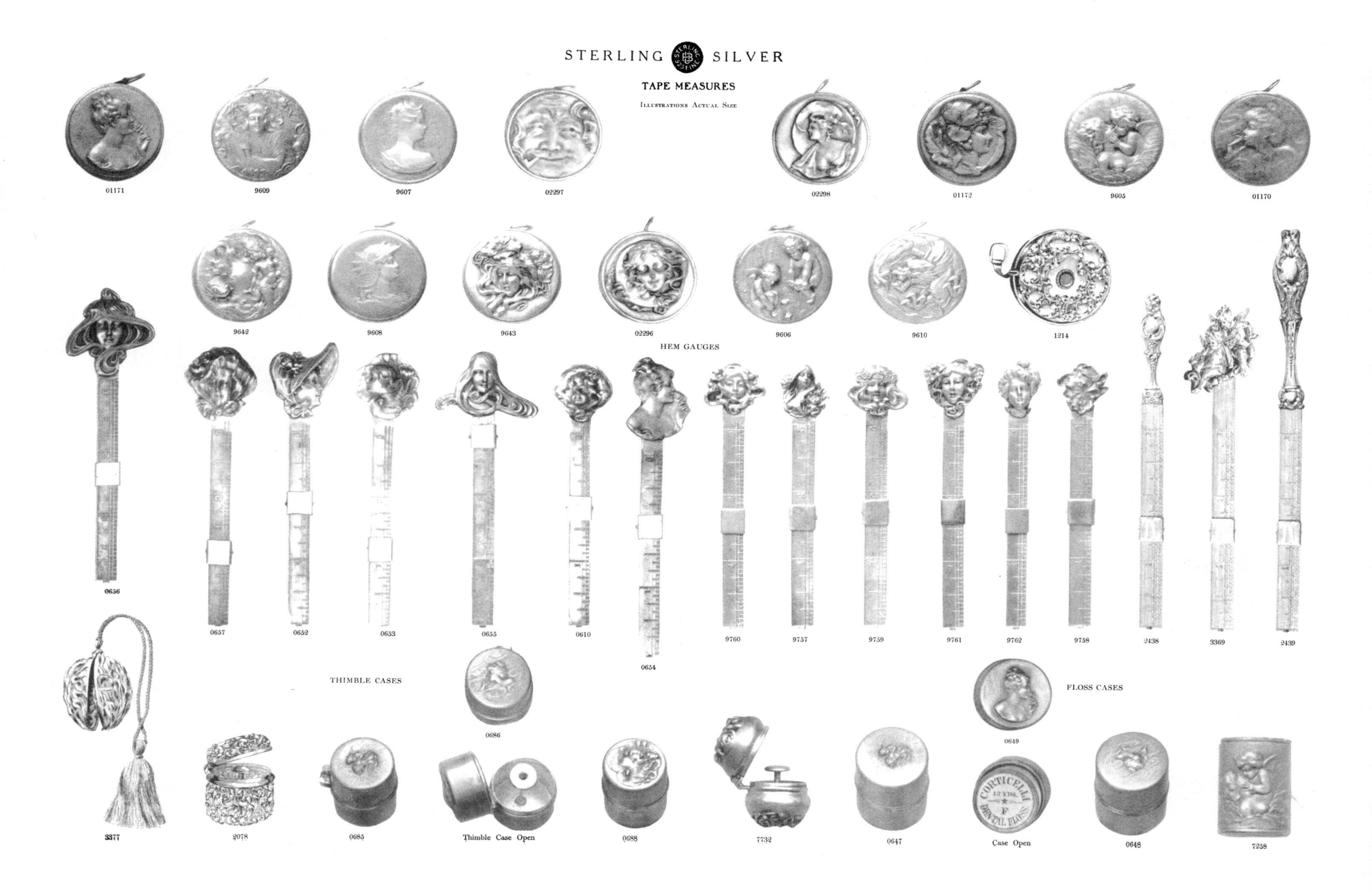

SEWING ARTICLES

Illustrations Actual Size

EMERIES

2380

2706

1875

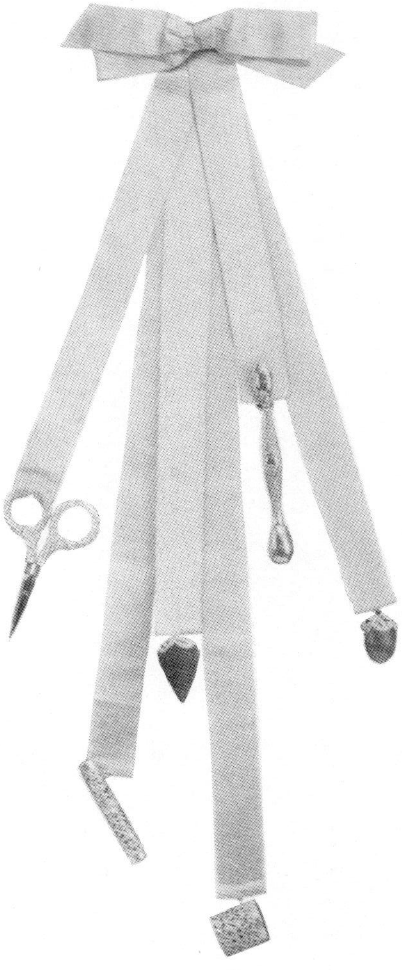

2695
Necessaire

531
Necessaire

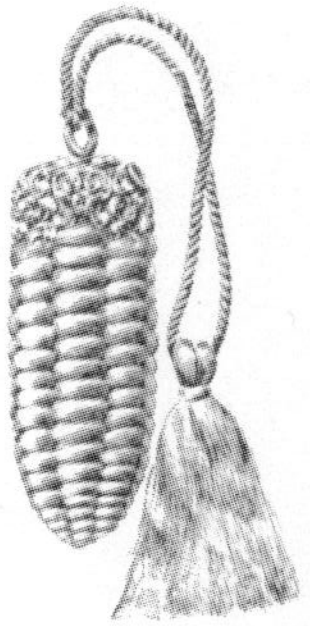

WAX BALLS

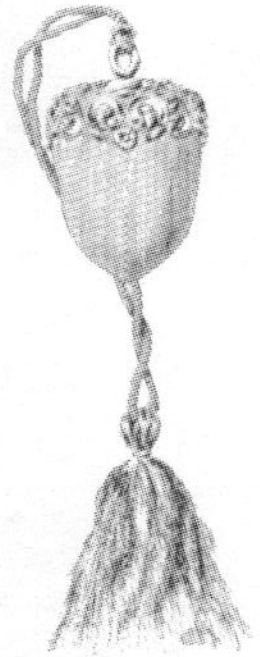

4034

2062

4036

4035

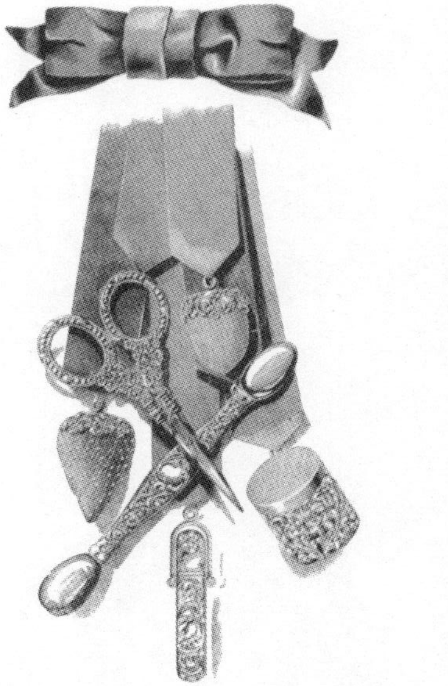

2696
Necessaire

6956

5956
Needle Cases

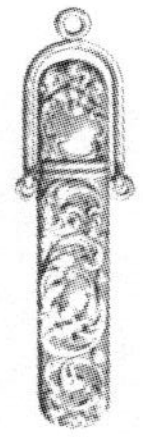

2036

1626
Needle Case

2397
Glove Darner

STERLING SILVER

PUFF JARS AND SOAP BOXES

Illustrations Actual Size

Lily
0965 Puff Jar, Prism
0966 Puff Jar, Newark
02409 Soap Jar

He Loves Me
10000 Puff Jar, Prism
01 Puff Jar, Newark
01053 Soap Jar

Reine des Fleurs
0678 Puff Jar, Prism
0679 Puff Jar, Newark
01378 Soap Jar

Old English
0974 Puff Jar, Prism
0975 Puff Jar, Newark
02410 Soap Jar

Les Secrete des Fleurs
0669 Puff Jar, Prism
0670 Puff Jar, Newark
01377 Soap Jar

Evangeline
9984 Puff Jar, Prism
9985 Puff Jar, Newark
01054 Soap Jar

Peep-o'-Day
0660 Puff Jar, Prism
0661 Puff Jar, Newark
01376 Soap Jar

Love's Dream
6141 Puff Jar, Prism
6152 Puff Jar, Newark
01051 Soap Jar

Dawn
9992 Puff Jar, Prism
9993 Puff Jar, Newark
01052 Soap Jar

Newark Jar

Indian
6362 Puff Jar, Prism
6363 Puff Jar, Newark
01055 Soap Jar

Shaving Soap Jar

Love's Voyage
6452 Puff Jar, Prism
6453 Puff Jar, Newark

Prism Jar

STERLING SILVER

JARS

Illustrations Actual Size

Stolen Kiss
0959 Vaseline Jar
0960 Talcum Bottle
0963 Hair Pin Bottle
0962 Tooth Powder Bottle
0961 Tooth Brush Bottle

Lily
0968 Vaseline Jar
0969 Talcum Bottle
0972 Hair Pin Bottle
0971 Tooth Powder Bottle
0970 Tooth Brush Bottle

Old English
0977 Vaseline Jar
0978 Talcum Bottle
0981 Hair Pin Bottle
0980 Tooth Powder Bottle
0979 Tooth Brush Bottle

Les Secrete des Fleurs
0667 Vaseline Jar
0672 Talcum Bottle
0674 Hair Pin Bottle
0675 Tooth Powder Bottle
0673 Tooth Brush Bottle

He Loves Me
9998 Vaseline Jar
03 Talcum Bottle
05 Hair Pin Bottle
01239 Tooth Powder Bottle
04 Tooth Brush Bottle

Reine des Fleurs
0676 Vaseline Jar
0681 Talcum Bottle
0683 Hair Pin Bottle
0684 Tooth Powder Bottle
0682 Tooth Brush Bottle

Dawn
9990 Vaseline Jar
9995 Talcum Bottle
9997 Hair Pin Bottle
01238 Tooth Powder Bottle
9996 Tooth Brush Bottle

Evangeline
9982 Vaseline Jar
9987 Talcum Bottle
9989 Hair Pin Bottle
01237 Tooth Powder Bottle
9988 Tooth Brush Bottle

Love's Dream
6368 Vaseline Jar
8783 Talcum Bottle
6361 Hair Pin Bottle
0431 Tooth Powder Bottle
6365 Tooth Brush Bottle

Peep-o'-Day
0658 Vaseline Jar
0663 Talcum Bottle
0665 Hair Pin Bottle
0666 Tooth Powder Bottle
0664 Tooth Brush Bottle

Love's Voyage
8343 Vaseline Jar

Chilly Cupids
9693 Vaseline Jar

Art Nouveau
8344 Vaseline Jar

Waterlily
9980 Vaseline Jar Top

Narcissus
3847 Vaseline Jar

Apple Blossom
6303 Vaseline Jar

Rose
6304 Vaseline Jar

Fox Chase
6128 Vaseline Jar, Prism

Love's Dream
6129 Vaseline Jar, Prism

Vaseline Jar

Love's Voyage
8341 Large Talcum Powder Jar

Hair Pin Bottle

Love's Dream
6359 Large Talcum Powder Jar

Prism Jar

Steeplechase
6127 Vaseline Jar, Prism

Caddie Boy
6132 Vaseline Jar, Prism

Tooth Powder Bottle

Tooth Brush Bottle

Talcum Jar

Chilly Cupids
6360 Large Talcum Powder Jar

Large Talcum Powder Jar

STERLING SILVER

INK WELLS

6257 Golf Player

6258 Love's Dream

6259 Chilly Cupids

6253 Love's Dream

045 Indian

8333 Love's Dream

6254 Golf Player

6264 Rose
6263 "
6267 "
6268 "

6265 Apple Blossom
6262 " "
6260 " "

6266 Rose
6261 "

6267 Rose Top

6265 Apple Blossom Top
6266 Rose Top

6257 Golf Player Top
6258 Love's Dream Top
6259 Chilly Cupids Top

6254 Golf Player Top
045 Indian
8333 Love's Dream

6253 Love's Dream Top

6268 Rose Top

6264 Rose Top

6262 Apple Blossom Top
6263 Rose Top

6260 Apple Blossom Top
6261 Rose Top

STERLING SILVER

PUNGENTS

Illustrations Actual Size

Cologne Bottle
6271 Apple Blossom Top
6272 Rose Top

6291 Rose Top

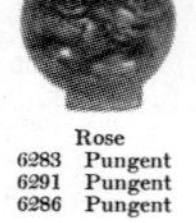

Rose
6283 Pungent
6291 Pungent
6286 Pungent

6286 Rose Top

Apple Blossom
6271 Cologne Bottle
6269 Cologne Bottle
6282 Pungent

6283 Rose Top

Rose
6289 Pungent

Rose
6281 Pungent
6272 Cologne Bottle
6270 Cologne Bottle

6281 Rose Top
6282 Apple Blossom Top

6289 Rose Top

Cologne Bottle
6270 Rose Top
6269 Apple Blossom Top

Salts Jar
2318 Chased Top
6273 Chilly Cupids Top
6274 Fox Chase Top

Cigarette Jar
6296 Love's Dream Top
6295 Golf Player Top

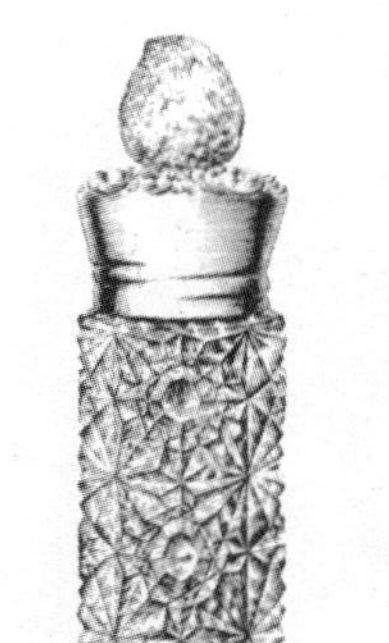

3854
Stamp Moistener

Cigarette Jar
6294 Mermaid Top
6293 Fox Chase Top

Salts Jar
2365 Chased Top
6275 Golf Player Top
6276 Love's Dream Top

Silver Stopper
Chilly Cupids

2514 Tooth Powder Bottle

3843 Tooth Powder Bottle

6398 Hair Receiver

3784 Talcum Powder Jar

6347—7687 Cologne Bottle

Other Sizes with Silver Stoppers

Chilly Cupids Top 7687—6347—Capacity 28 oz.
Chilly Cupids Top 7686—6348—Capacity 16 oz.
Love's Dream Top 7685—6349—Capacity 10 oz.
Chilly Cupids Top 7684—6350—Capacity 8 oz.
Rose Top 7683—6351—Capacity 4 oz.
Reine des Fleurs Top 01923—6349—Capacity 10 oz.
Le Secrete des Fleurs Top 01924—6349—Capacity 10 oz.
Peep-o'-Day Top 01925—6349—Capacity 10 oz.

2234 Mucilage Jar

3361 $10\frac{1}{2}$ inches high

3844 Glove Powder Bottle

3755